At any time, we could all stop paying rent, mortgages, taxes, utilities; they would be powerless against us if we all quit at once. At any time, we could all stop going to work or school—or go to them and refuse to obey orders or leave the premises, instead turning them into community centers. At any time, we could tear up our IDs, take the license plates off our cars, cut down security cameras, burn money, throw away our wallets, and assemble cooperative associations to produce and distribute everything we need.

Whenever my shift drags, I find myself thinking about this stuff. Am I really the only person who's ever had this idea? I can imagine all the usual objections, but you can bet if it took off in some part of the world everybody else would get in on it quick. Think of the unspeakable ways we're all wasting our lives instead. What would it take to get that chain reaction started? Where do I go to meet people who don't just hate their jobs, but are ready to be done with work once and for all?

WO

CrimethInc. Workers' Collective ∫ Salem, OR ∫ Two Thousand Eleven

N©!2011 CrimethInc. ex-Workers' Collective;
property is theft—steal it back
CrimethInc. Far East,
P.O. Box 13998,
Salem, OR 97309-1998
inquiries@crimethinc.com

The diagram of the pyramid of capitalist society is by
Packard Jennings: centennialsociety.com

A full-size electronic version of the diagram and an array of
poster designs are available here: **www.crimethinc.com/work**

You can obtain a printed version of the diagram, along with a
great deal of other material, via **www.crimethinc.com**

Printed in Canada by unionized printers
on 100% post-consumer recycled paper.

"Is it conceivable that there can be a 'fair market price,' or any price whatsoever, estimable in gold, or diamonds, or bank notes, or government bonds, for a man's [sic] supremest possession—that one possession without which his life is totally worthless—his liberty?"

– Mark Twain

By itself,
this is a book about work,
but it's also more than that.

It complements a diagram of the different positions and dynamics that make up the economy that necessitates work. Together, the book and diagram outline an analysis of capitalism: what it is, how it works, how we might dismantle it. And the book, the diagram, and the analysis are all outgrowths of something more—a movement of people determined to fight it.

So this book isn't just an attempt to describe reality but also a tool with which to change it. If any of the words or illustrations resonate with you, don't leave them trapped on these pages—write them on the wall, shout them over the intercom at your former workplace, change them as you see fit and release them into the world. You can find poster versions of many of the illustrations at **crimethinc.com/work** for this purpose.

This project is the combined effort of a group of people who have already spent many years in pitched struggle against capitalism. What qualifies us to write this? Some of us used to be students or pizza deliverers or dishwashers; others still are construction workers or graphic designers or civic-minded criminals. But all of us have lived under capitalism since we were born, and that makes us experts on it. The same goes for you. No one has to have a degree in economics to understand what's happening: it's enough to get a paycheck or a pink slip and *pay attention.* We're suspicious of the experts who get their credentials from on high, who have incentives to minimize things that are obvious to everyone else.

Like every attempt to construct a scale model of the world, this one is bound to be partial in both senses of the word. To present the whole story, it would have to be as vast as history. There's no way to be unbiased, either: our positions and values inevitably influence what we include and what we leave out. What we offer here is simply one perspective from our side of the counter and our side of the barricades. If it lines up with yours, *let's do something about it.*

better ashes than dust—
CrimethInc. Workers' Collective

Mechanics: *How It Works*

At this moment, an employee in a grocery store is setting
   out genetically engineered produce rather than
   tending her garden;

A dishwasher is sweating over a steaming sink while
   unwashed dishes stack up in his kitchen;

A line cook is taking orders from strangers instead of
   cooking at a neighborhood barbecue;

An advertising agent is composing jingles for laundry
   detergent rather than playing music with his friends;

A woman is watching wealthier people's children at a
   daycare program rather than spending time with her own;

A child is being dropped off there instead of growing up
   with those who know and love him;

A student is writing a thesis about an activity that interests
   her instead of participating in it;

A man is masturbating with internet pornography instead
   of exploring his sexuality with a partner;

An activist, weary after a hard day's work, is putting on a
   Hollywood movie for entertainment;

And a demonstrator who has her own unique reasons
   to protest is carrying a sign mass-produced by a
   bureaucratic organization.

I. The Occupation

Occupation. The word brings to mind images of Russian tanks rolling through the streets of Eastern Europe, or US soldiers nervously patrolling hostile neighborhoods in the Middle East.

But not every occupation is so obvious. Sometimes occupations go on so long the tanks become unnecessary. They can be rolled back into storage, as long as the conquered remember they can return at any time—or behave as if the tanks were still there, forgetting why they do so.

How do you recognize an occupation? Historically, occupied peoples had to pay a tribute to their conquerors, or else render them some kind of service. A tribute is a sort of rent the occupied pay just to live on their own lands; and as for the service—well, what's *your* occupation? You know, what occupies your time? A job, probably, or two—or preparations for one, or recovery from one, or looking for one. You need that

job to pay your rent or mortgage, among other things—but wasn't the building you live in built by people like yourself, people who had to work to pay their rent too? The same goes for all those other products you have to earn money to pay for—you and others like you made them, but you have to buy them from companies like the one that employs you, companies that neither pay you all the money they make from your labor nor sell their products at the price it cost to produce them. They're getting you coming and going!

Our lives are occupied territory. Who controls the resources in your community, who shapes your neighborhood and the landscape around it, who sets your schedule day by day and month by month? Even if you're self-employed, are *you* the one who decides what you have to do to make money? Picture your idea of perfect bliss—does it bear a suspicious resemblance to the utopias you see in advertisements?

Not only our time, but also our ambitions, our sexuality, our values, our very sense of what it means to be human—all these are occupied, molded according to the demands of the market.

And we aren't the only territory under enemy control. The invisible occupation of our lives mirrors the military occupation of areas at the fringe of this conquered land, where guns and tanks are still necessary to enforce the property rights of robber barons and the liberty of corporations to trade at the expense of hostile locals—some of whom still remember what life is like without leases, salaries, or bosses.

You might not be all that different from them yourself, despite having been raised in captivity. Maybe in the boss's office, or in career counseling or romantic quarrels, whenever someone was trying to command your attention and your attention wouldn't cooperate, you've been chided for being *preoccupied*. That is—some rebel part of you is still held by daydreams and fantasies, lingering hopes that your life could somehow be more than an *occupation*.

There *is* a rebel army out in the bush plotting the abolition of wage slavery, as sure as there are employees in every workplace waging guerrilla war with loafing, pilfering, and disobedience—and you can join up, too, if you haven't already. But before we start laying plans and sharpening spears, let's look more closely at what we're up against.

i. Work

What exactly is work? We could define it as *activity for the sake of making money*. But aren't slave labor and unpaid internships work, too? We could say it's activity that accumulates profit for *someone*, whether or not it benefits the one who carries it out. But does that mean that as soon as you start making money from an activity, it becomes work even if it was *play* before? Perhaps we could define work as labor that takes more from us than it gives back, or that is governed by external forces.

Or perhaps we can only understand what work is by stepping back to look at the context in which it takes place. In a world of "diversity," one common thread connects us: we're all subject to the economy. Christian or Muslim, communist or conservative, in São Paulo or St. Paul, you probably have to spend the better part of your life trading time for money, or make someone else do it for you, or suffer the consequences.

What else can you do? If you refuse, the economy will go on without you; it doesn't need you any more than it needs any of the hundreds of millions already unemployed, and there's no point going hungry for nothing. You can join a co-op or commune, but you'll still face the same market pressures. You can canvas and lobby and protest on behalf of sweatshop workers, but even if you succeed in getting reforms passed, they—like you—will still have to work, whether in maquiladoras or NGO offices. You can go out at night in a black mask and smash all the windows of the shopping district, but the next day you'll have to do your shopping somewhere. You could make a million dollars and *still* be stuck with your nose at the grindstone trying to keep your lead on everyone else. Even when workers overthrew governments to establish communist utopias, they ended up back at work—if they were lucky.

All this makes it easy to feel that work is inevitable, that there's no other way our lives could be structured. That's convenient for the ones who profit most from this arrangement: they don't have to prove that it's the *best* system if everyone thinks it's the only one *possible*. Is this really how life has always been?

Now, however, even the future of the economy is uncertain.

Forget about the Economy—What about Us?

When the economy crashes, politicians and pundits bewail the consequences for average working families. They demand emergency measures—such as giving billions of dollars of taxpayer money to the banks that caused the crisis by ripping off "average working families" in the first place. What's going on here?

We're told that our lives depend on the economy, that it's worth any sacrifice to keep it running. But for most of us, keeping it running is *always* a sacrifice.

When the economy crashes, mining companies stop blowing up mountains. Developers stop cutting down forests to build new offices and condominiums. Factories stop pouring pollutants into rivers. Gentrification grinds to a halt. Workaholics reconsider their priorities. Prisons are forced to release inmates. Police departments can't buy new weapons. Governments can't afford to mass-arrest demonstrators. Sheriffs sometimes even refuse to evict families from foreclosed homes.

Of course, millions more are forced out of their homes and go hungry. But the problem isn't that there's no housing or food to be had—it's not the *crisis* that causes that, but the fact that the system is still functioning. Long before the crash, people were being forced out of their homes while buildings stood empty and going hungry while food surpluses rotted. If more people go hungry during a recession, it's not because there has been any material change in our productive capacities, but simply one more example of how irrationally our society *always* distributes resources.

When workers go on strike, you can see some of the same effects as during a crash. They may go hungry, but they can also develop a new awareness of their power as they get to know each other outside the constraints of the daily grind. The rest of society suddenly notices that they exist. Sometimes they establish new collective projects and ways of making decisions. Occasionally they even take over their workplaces and use them to do things outside the logic of profit and competition. The same goes for student occupations.

So perhaps the real issue is that crashes and strikes don't go *far enough*. So long as the economy runs our lives, any interruption is going to be hard on us; but even if nothing ever went wrong, it would never deliver the world of our dreams.

And whether or not we're ready for change, things aren't going to go on this way forever. Who can still believe we're on the right track now that pollution is killing off species by the thousand and causing the polar ice caps to melt? Between global warming and nuclear war, industrial capitalism has already produced at least two different ways of *ending life on earth*. That doesn't sound very stable!

If we want to survive another century, we have to reexamine the mythology that grounds our current way of life.

The MYTHOLOGY of WORK

What if nobody worked? Sweatshops would empty out and assembly lines would grind to a halt, at least the ones producing things no one would make voluntarily. Telemarketing would cease. Despicable individuals who only hold sway over others because of wealth and title would have to learn better social skills. Traffic jams would come to an end; so would oil spills. Paper money and job applications would be used as fire starter as people reverted to barter and sharing. Grass and flowers would grow from the cracks in the sidewalk, eventually making way for fruit trees.

And we would all starve to death. But we're not exactly subsisting on paperwork and performance evaluations, are we? Most of the things we make and do for money are patently irrelevant to our survival— and to what gives life meaning, besides.

WORK IS NECESSARY.

That depends on what you mean by "work." Think about how many people enjoy gardening, fishing, carpentry, cooking, and even computer programming just for their own sake. What if that kind of activity could provide for all our needs?

For hundreds of years, people have claimed that technological progress would soon liberate humanity from the need to work. Today we have capabilities our ancestors couldn't have imagined, but those predictions still haven't come true. In the US we actually work longer hours than we did a couple generations ago—the poor in order to survive, the rich in order to compete. Others desperately seek employment, hardly enjoying the comfortable leisure all this progress should provide. Despite the talk of recession and the need for austerity measures, corporations are reporting record earnings, the wealthiest are wealthier than ever, and tremendous quantities of goods are produced just to be thrown away. There's plenty of wealth, but it's not being used to liberate humanity.

What kind of system simultaneously produces abundance and prevents us from making the most of it? The defenders of the free market argue that there's no other option—and so long as our society is organized this way, there isn't.

Yet once upon a time, before time cards and power lunches, everything got done without work. The natural world that provided for our needs hadn't yet been carved up and privatized. Knowledge and skills weren't the exclusive domains of licensed experts, held hostage by expensive institutions; time wasn't divided into productive work and consumptive leisure. We know this because work was invented only a few thousand years ago, but human beings have been around for hundreds of thousands of years. We're told that life was "solitary, poor, nasty, brutish, and short" back then—but that narrative comes to us from the ones who stamped out that way of life, not the ones who practiced it.

This isn't to say we should go back to the way things used to be, or that we could—only that things don't have to be the way they are right now. If our distant ancestors could see us today, they'd probably be excited about some of our inventions and horrified by others, but they'd surely be shocked by how we apply them. We built this world with our labor, and without certain obstacles we could surely build a better one. That wouldn't mean abandoning everything we've learned. It would just mean abandoning everything we've learned *doesn't work*.

WORK IS PRODUCTIVE.

One can hardly deny that work is productive. Just a couple thousand years
of it have dramatically transformed the
surface of the earth.

But what exactly does it produce? Disposable chopsticks
by the billion; laptops and cell phones that are obsolete
within a couple years. Miles of waste dumps and tons upon
tons of chlorofluorocarbons. Factories that will rust as soon
as labor is cheaper elsewhere. Dumpsters full of overstock,
while a billion suffer malnutrition; medical treatments only
the wealthy can afford; novels and philosophies and art
movements most of us just don't have time for in a society
that subordinates desires to profit motives and needs to
property rights.

And where do the resources for all this production come
from? What happens to the ecosystems and communities
that are pillaged and exploited? If work is productive, it's
even more *destructive*.

Work doesn't produce goods out of thin air; it's not
a conjuring act. Rather, it takes raw materials from the
biosphere—a common treasury shared by all living things—
and transforms them into products animated by the logic
of market. For those who see the world in terms of balance
sheets, this is an improvement, but the rest of us shouldn't
take their word for it.

Capitalists and socialists have always taken it for granted
that work produces value. Workers have to consider a
different possibility—that working *uses up* value. That's
why the forests and polar ice caps are being consumed
alongside the hours of our lives: the aches in our bodies

when we come home from work parallel the damage taking place on a global scale.

What should we be producing, if not all this stuff? Well, how about *happiness itself*? Can we imagine a society in which the primary goal of our activity was to make the most of life, to explore its mysteries, rather than to amass wealth or outflank competition? We would still make material goods in such a society, of course, but not in order to compete for profit. Festivals, feasts, philosophy, romance, creative pursuits, child-rearing, friendship, adventure—can we picture these as the center of life, rather than packed into our spare time?

Today things are the other way around—our conception of happiness is constructed as a means to stimulate *production*. Small wonder products are crowding us out of the world.

WORK CREATES WEALTH.

Work doesn't simply create wealth where there was only poverty before. On the contrary, so long as it enriches some at others' expense, work creates *poverty*, too, in direct proportion to profit.

Poverty is not an objective condition, but a relationship produced by unequal distribution of resources. There's no such thing as poverty in societies in which people share everything. There may be scarcity, but no one is subjected to the indignity of having to go without while others have more than they know what to do with. As profit is accumulated and the minimum threshold of wealth necessary to exert influence in society rises higher and higher, poverty becomes more and more debilitating. It is a form of exile—

the cruelest form of exile, for you stay within society while being excluded from it. You can neither participate nor go anywhere else.

Work doesn't just create poverty alongside wealth—it concentrates wealth in the hands of a few while spreading poverty far and wide. For every Bill Gates, a million people must live below the poverty line; for every Shell Oil, there has to be a Nigeria. The more we work, the more profit is accumulated from our labor, and the poorer we are compared to our exploiters.

So in addition to creating wealth, *work makes people poor*. This is clear even before we factor in all the *other* ways work makes us poor: poor in self-determination, poor in free time, poor in health, poor in sense of self beyond our careers and bank accounts, poor in spirit.

GOODNESS, GENTLEMEN, WE CAN'T *ALL* BE
BILLIONAIRES—THAT WOULD JUST BE *INFLATION.*
REALLY NOW! IF ANYONE IS TO BE RICH,
SOMEBODY HAS TO BE POOR.

YOU NEED TO WORK TO MAKE A LIVING.

"Cost of living" estimates are misleading—there's little living going on at all! "Cost of working" is more like it, and it's not cheap.

Everyone knows what housecleaners and dishwashers pay for being the backbone of our economy. All the scourges of poverty—addiction, broken families, poor health—are par for the course; the ones who survive these and somehow go on showing up on time are working miracles. Think what they could accomplish if they were free to apply that power to something other than earning profits for their employers!

What about their employers, fortunate to be higher on the pyramid? You would think earning a higher salary would mean having more money and thus more freedom, but it's not that simple. Every job entails hidden costs: just as a dishwasher has to pay bus fare to and from work every day, a corporate lawyer has to be able to fly anywhere at a moment's notice, to maintain a country club membership for informal business meetings, to own a small mansion in which to entertain dinner guests that double as clients. This is why it's so difficult for middle-class workers to save up enough money to quit while they're ahead and get out of the rat race: trying to get ahead in the economy basically means running in place. At best, you might advance to a fancier treadmill, but you'll have to run faster to stay on it.

And these merely financial costs of working are the least expensive. In one survey, people of all walks of life were asked how much money they would need to live the life they wanted; from pauper to patrician, they all answered approximately double whatever their current income was.

So not only is money costly to obtain, but, like any addictive drug, it's less and less fulfilling! And the further up you get in the hierarchy, the more you have to fight to hold your place. The wealthy executive must abandon his unruly passions and his conscience, must convince himself that he deserves more than the unfortunates whose labor provides for his comfort, must smother his every impulse to question, to share, to imagine himself in others' shoes; if he doesn't, sooner or later some more ruthless contender replaces him. Both blue collar and white collar workers have to kill themselves to keep the jobs that keep them alive; it's just a question of physical or spiritual destruction.

Those are the costs we pay individually, but there's also a global price to pay for all this working. Alongside the environmental costs, there are work-related illnesses, injuries, and deaths: every year we kill people by the thousand to sell hamburgers and health club memberships to the survivors. The US Department of Labor reported that twice as many people suffered fatal work injuries in 2001 as died in the September 11 attacks, and that doesn't begin to take into account work-related illnesses. Above all, more exorbitant than any other price, there is the cost of never learning how to direct our own lives, never getting the chance to answer or even ask the question of what we would do with our time on this planet if it was up to us. We can never know how much we are giving up by settling for a world in which people are too busy, too poor, or too beaten down to do so.

Why work, if it's so expensive? Everyone knows the answer—there's no other way to acquire the resources we need to survive, or for that matter to participate in society at all. All the earlier social forms that made other ways of life possible have been eradicated—they were stamped out by conquistadors, slave traders, and corporations that left neither tribe nor tradition nor ecosystem intact. Contrary to capitalist propaganda, free human beings don't crowd into factories for a pittance if they have other options, not even in return for name brand shoes and software.

In working and shopping and paying bills, each of us helps perpetuate the conditions that necessitate these activities. Capitalism exists because we invest everything in it: all our energy and ingenuity in the marketplace, all our resources at the supermarket and in the stock market, all our attention in the media. To be more precise, capitalism exists because our daily activities *are* it. But would we continue to reproduce it if we felt we had another choice?

"A slow sort of country!" said the Queen. "Now **here**, you see, it takes all the running **you** can do, to keep in the same place. If you want to get somewhere else, you must run at least twice as fast as that."

"I'd rather not try, please!" said Alice.

WORK IS A PATH TO FULFILLMENT.

On the contrary, instead of enabling people to achieve happiness, work fosters the worst kind of self-denial.

Obeying teachers, bosses, the demands of the market—not to mention laws, parents' expectations, religious scriptures, social norms—we're conditioned from infancy to put our desires on hold. Following orders becomes an unconscious reflex, whether or not they are in our best interest; deferring to experts becomes second nature.

Selling our time rather than doing things for their own sake, we come to evaluate our lives on the basis of how much we can get in exchange for them, not what we get out of them. As freelance slaves hawking our lives hour by hour, we think of ourselves as each having a price; the amount of the price becomes our measure of value. In that sense, we become commodities, just like toothpaste and toilet paper. What once was a human being is now an employee, in the same way that what once was a pig is now a pork chop. Our lives disappear, spent like the money for which we trade them.

Often we become so used to giving up things that are precious to us that *sacrifice* comes to be our only way of expressing that we care about something. We martyr ourselves for ideas, causes, love of one another, even when these are supposed to help us find happiness.

There are families, for example, in which people show affection by competing to be the one who gives up the most for the others. Gratification isn't just delayed, it's passed on from one generation to the next. The responsibility of finally enjoying all the happiness presumably saved up over years of thankless toil is deferred to the children; yet when they come of age, if they are to be seen as responsible adults, they too must begin working their fingers to the bone.

But the buck has to stop somewhere.

> ## "If hard work were such a wonderful thing, surely the rich would have kept it all to themselves."
> – Lane Kirkland

WORK INSTILLS INITIATIVE.

People work hard nowadays, that's for sure. Tying access to resources to market performance has caused unprecedented production and technological progress. Indeed, the market has monopolized access to our own creative capacities to such an extent that many people work not only to survive but also to *have something to do*. But what kind of initiative does this instill?

Let's go back to global warming, one of the most serious crises facing the planet. After decades of denial, politicians and businessmen have finally swung into action to do something about it. And what are they doing? Casting about for ways to cash in! Carbon credits, "clean" coal, "green" investment firms—who believes that these are the *most effective* way to curb the production of greenhouse gases? It's ironic that a catastrophe caused by capitalist consumerism can be used to spur more consumption, but it reveals a lot about the kind of initiative work instills. What kind of person, confronted with the task of preventing the end of life on earth, responds, "Sure, but what's in it for *me?*"

If everything in our society has to be driven by a profit motive to succeed, that might not be initiative after all, but something else. Really taking initiative, initiating new values and new modes of behavior—this is as unthinkable to the enterprising businessman as it is to his most listless employee. What if working—that is, leasing your creative powers to others, whether managers or customers—actually *erodes* initiative?

The evidence for this extends beyond the workplace. How many people who never miss a day of work can't show up on time for band practice? We can't keep up with the reading for our book clubs even when we can finish papers for school on time; the things we *really* want to do with our lives end up at the bottom of the to-do list. The ability to follow through on commitments becomes something outside ourselves, associated with external rewards or punishments.

Imagine a world in which everything people did, they did because they *wanted* to, because they were personally invested in bringing it about. For any boss who has struggled to motivate indifferent employees, the idea of working with people who are equally invested in the same projects sounds utopian. But this isn't proof that nothing would get done without bosses and salaries—it just shows how work saps us of initiative.

WORK PROVIDES SECURITY.

Let's say your job never injures, poisons, or sickens you. Let's also take it for granted that the economy doesn't crash and take your job and savings with it, and that no one who got a worse deal than you manages to hurt or rob you. You still can't be sure you won't be downsized. Nowadays nobody works for the same employer his whole life; you work somewhere a few years until they let you go for someone younger and cheaper or outsource your job overseas. You can break your back to prove you're the best in your field and still end up hung out to dry.

You have to count on your employers to make shrewd decisions so they can write your paycheck—they can't just fritter money away or they won't have it to pay you. But you never know when that shrewdness will turn against you: the ones you depend on for your livelihood didn't get where they are by being sentimental. If you're self-employed, you probably know how fickle the market can be, too.

What could provide real security? Perhaps being part of a long-term community in which people looked out for each other, a community based on mutual assistance rather than financial incentives. And what is one of the chief obstacles to building that kind of community today? *Work.*

ca·reer (kə-rîr´) *v. –intr.* **1.** Move swiftly and in an uncontrolled way in a specified direction: *the car careered across the road and went through a hedge.*

WORK TEACHES RESPONSIBILITY.

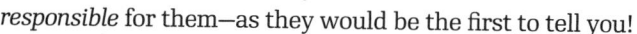

Who carried out most of the injustices in history? *Employees.* This is not necessarily to say they are *responsible* for them—as they would be the first to tell you!

Does receiving a wage absolve you of responsibility for your actions? Working seems to foster the impression that it does. The Nuremburg defense—"I was just following orders"—has been the anthem and alibi of millions of employees. This willingness to check one's conscience at the workplace door—to be, in fact, a mercenary—lies at the root of many of the troubles plaguing our species.

People have done horrible things without orders, too—but not nearly so many horrible things. You can reason with a person who is acting for herself; she acknowledges that she is accountable for her decisions. Employees, on the other hand, can do unimaginably dumb and destructive things while refusing to think about the consequences.

The real problem, of course, isn't employees refusing to take responsibility for their actions—it's the economic system that makes taking responsibility so prohibitively expensive.

NOTICE

Employees must wash hands of responsibility before returning to work.

Employees dump toxic waste into rivers and oceans.

Employees slaughter cows and perform experiments on monkeys.

Employees throw away truckloads of food.

Employees are destroying the ozone layer.

They watch your every move through security cameras.

They evict you when you don't pay your rent.

They imprison you when you don't pay your taxes.

They humiliate you when you don't do your homework or show up to work on time.

They enter information about your private life into credit reports and FBI files.

They give you speeding tickets and tow your car.

They administer standardized exams, juvenile detention centers, and lethal injections.

The soldiers who herded people into gas chambers were employees,

Just like the soldiers occupying Iraq and Afghanistan,

Just like the suicide bombers who target them—they are employees of God, hoping to be paid in paradise.

THAT'S ENOUGH!

**YOU HAVE TO PAY YOUR OWN WAY—
EVEN IF THAT MEANS DOING IT AT
EVERYONE ELSE'S EXPENSE!
ANYTHING ELSE IS IRRESPONSIBLE,
SUICIDAL, A SIN AGAINST GOD,
A BETRAYAL OF YOUR POOR PARENTS,
A SLAP IN THE FACE OF ALL THE POOR
BASTARDS WHO HAVE NO OTHER CHOICE,
AND A VIOLATION OF THE
TERMS OF YOUR PROBATION—
NOT TO MENTION PROOF THAT YOU MUST
BE A SPOILED BRAT WITH A TRUST FUND!**

NOW GET BACK IN THERE AND GO BACK TO WORK!

Let's be clear about this—critiquing work doesn't mean rejecting labor, effort, ambition, or commitment. It doesn't mean demanding that everything be fun or easy. Fighting against the forces that compel us to work is hard work. Laziness is not the alternative to work, though it might be a *byproduct* of it.

The bottom line is simple: all of us deserve to make the most of our potential as we see fit, to be the masters of our own destinies. Being forced to sell these things away to survive is tragic and humiliating. *We don't have to live like this.*

ii. The Economy

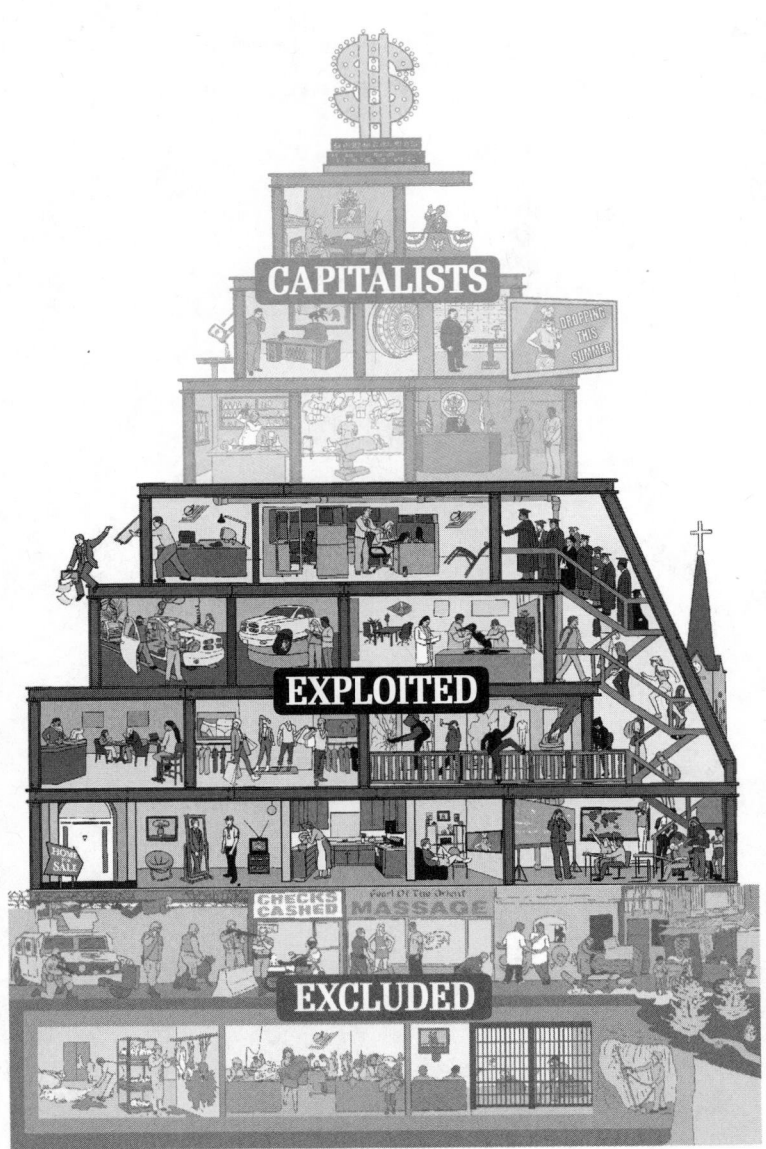

Understanding The Economy

The economy extends infinitely in all directions around us. It seems impossible to get a handle on how it works. How could anyone conceptualize the activities of billions of human beings?

The idea that you need *a complete understanding of the economy* to come to any conclusions about it just serves to silence people. By that reasoning, only the best-informed economists are entitled to decide whether to go to work in the morning. However informed we are, at every moment we all have to choose whether to continue what we've been doing or try something else.

Perhaps instead we can start from our individual positions, looking at the things that are familiar to us. If there are general principles that govern capitalism, they should be visible from wherever we begin. In this view, an economist isn't necessarily more qualified to talk about the economy than a janitor.

There are many ways to structure an analysis of the economy. One conventional approach is to break it into sectors according to the processes of production and consumption: sector one involves direct resource extraction such as mining and agriculture, sector two includes manufacturing and construction, sector three is the service industry, and so on.

In the 19th century over two thirds of US laborers worked in the primary sector; today, over 80% of the labor force is employed in the tertiary sector.

But if we want to focus on who benefits from the current state of affairs, it makes more sense to divide things up according to other criteria. Studying the flows of capital, we might say there are three basic categories: **capitalists**, who profit from others' labor; the **exploited**, whose activity turns a profit for others; and the **excluded**, who are left out of the equation and have to survive on the fringes of the economy. These categories are not exclusive or definitive; some people occupy multiple positions at once or during different phases of their lives.

Capitalists make money not only on what they *do*, but also from what they own. It takes money to make money, as the saying goes. Business owners, landlords, and large shareholders are capitalists. So are executives who receive salaries padded with money produced by other people's efforts. An employee who owns a small amount of company stock could be called a microcapitalist.

Capitalists derive their profit from the activity of the **exploited.** The majority of the exploited can only make money from their own labor, so it's easy for employers to pay them less than the value they produce. When banks and credit card companies make money off debtors, they're exploiting them, the same as a corporation that pays an employee a dollar to make a $200 pair of shoes.

Untold millions are at the mercy of the economy but **excluded** from participating in it. The unemployed and the homeless are excluded, along with most of the occupants of favelas and shantytowns around the world. Prisoners are often both excluded and exploited, being forced to work at a pittance that amounts to slave labor. Being excluded is not the same as being outside the market—the dispossessed are poor precisely because they are *inside* capitalism.

This is only one version of the story, of course. A horror movie buff might use different language: *vampires, robots, zombies.* We could also structure our analysis in terms of production and consumption, or material versus immaterial labor. And alongside these economic structures are other power structures, like race and gender, that can be charted countless other ways. The economy cannot be understood apart from these—could modern capitalism have come about without the colonialism that plundered the so-called New World? How about the racism that justified slavery, or the sexism expressed in glass ceilings and unpaid domestic labor? Nor can these be remedied without changing the economy. How much difference does it make to have an African-American president when nearly a million black men are behind bars?

So all these dynamics can't be disentangled or reduced to a single narrative. A real working model of the world would be as immense and complex as the world itself. The point is to develop tools that can help us make sense of our lives and regain control of them.

To that end, let's chart some of the economic roles and relationships that are familiar to us. This is just one cross-section of the economy—but if our hypothesis is correct, it should offer a starting point from which to understand our situation.

Shifting Terrain

The structure of the economy isn't static. It is constantly evolving and expanding, incorporating new territories, subjects, and modes of production and consumption. We can't rely on previous conceptions of it for guidance, although they can help us understand the ways it has changed over the years.

Resistance is one of the most powerful forces that drives the development of the economy. As people find new ways to fight or escape the roles imposed on them, the economy changes to suppress, incorporate, or outmode their resistance. One generation declares that industrialism is polluting the earth; the next generation sees "sustainability" become a selling point for new commodities. One generation rejects network television as an immobilizing spectacle controlled by an elite; the next becomes dependent on participatory formats such as Youtube and Facebook.

This means we can't just make incremental reforms over time. If employees win wage increases, landlords just raise their rent; if laws are passed to protect the environment, corporations take their business elsewhere.

It also makes it difficult to build up a resistance movement over the years. Often, as soon as a movement starts to pick up steam, the context changes and its sources of strength dry up. On the other hand, this volatility means that things sometimes change quickly and unexpectedly—and history is moving faster than ever these days.

CHECKS
CASHED

Pearl Of The Orient

MASSAGE

OPEN

The Metropolis

The economy reshapes the physical and social terrain in its own image: silicon valleys, motor cities, banana republics. It erases the distinction between natural and synthetic: a cornfield in Iowa is no more natural than the concrete wasteland of Newark, New Jersey. It unifies space while producing new partitions within it.

The metropolis in which our story takes place is *every* metropolis, which is to say it is *one* metropolis. Roses picked on plantations in rural Ecuador are sold to Manhattan businessmen the same day; a set by a DJ at a Barcelona nightclub is broadcast simultaneously in Johannesburg. News, fashions, and ideas are transmitted instantaneously around the globe; every city is populated by tourists and refugees from every other city. People spend more time communicating across hundreds of miles than they do talking to their neighbors. Physical distance between people in different cities is giving way to social distance between people *in the same city*.

National boundaries are increasingly obsolete as a framework for understanding economics. One can no longer distinguish the domestic economy from the global economy, if such a thing was ever possible. The majority of the wealth of many US corporations is comprised of their holdings overseas; a single task may be outsourced from New York

City to Mumbai; an idea from Argentina generates profits in Finland. The world isn't made up of distinct physical territories or political bodies; it is a sea of interlocking relations that, like wind, water, and thermal currents, do not conform to imaginary boundaries.

And yet, though national borders cannot block them, the economy imposes real constraints on these relations. Today the significant borders are not the horizontal ones drawn between regions but the vertical ones dividing social strata, which are enforced everywhere at once rather than at individual checkpoints. These divide the metropolis into different zones of privilege, determining access to resources and power. Such zones may meet anywhere: an undocumented immigrant cleans a congressman's house for illegally low wages; guards brandish guns at the gate of an expensive hotel housing European businessmen right next to a shantytown in New Delhi.

Work reshapes the world in its own image.

At the Top

Who wields the ultimate power in the capitalist system?

Is it heads of state? They seem to rule only at the behest of the wealthy, whose interests they protect. Is it the wealthiest ones, the magnates who own corporations and draw profit from a hundred shrewd investments? They still have to scramble to maintain their positions as a thousand contenders struggle to replace them. How about the Federal Reserve, the bankers, the ones who administrate the system? When something goes awry, they seem as powerless and distraught as everyone else. Is it a secret conspiracy of tycoons or Freemasons? That sounds like lingering anti-Semitic rhetoric, implying that the problem is the power of a specific group rather than the dynamics of the system itself.

Or is *no one* in control? People speak about the economy the way they speak about God or Nature, even though it's comprised of their own activities and the activities of people like them. It is a sort of Ouija board on which the self-interested actions of competing individuals add up to collective disempowerment. Has there ever been an autocrat as tyrannical and destructive as the market?

Capital appears to be autonomous. It flows one way, then another; it concentrates itself in one nation, then disappears capriciously overseas. From an economist's perspective, it is the subject of history, acting upon us. Its movements seem unstoppable, inevitable, a sort of financial weather. And yet capital as we know it is simply a collective hallucination imposed on the world, a socially produced relationship.

What is capital? Broadly put, it is a product of previous labor that can be used to produce wealth. This can take many forms. A factory is capital; a trademarked computer program can function as capital; if you have enough money left to play the stock market after you've paid your gas bill, that counts as capital too. The common thread is that all of these can be used to accumulate profit on an ongoing basis in a society that believes in private property. Capitalism is the system in which private ownership of capital determines the social landscape: in a sense, it really is *capital* that calls the shots, ruling through interchangeable human hosts.

That doesn't mean the solution is to use political structures to "tame" capital, making it more rational, more "democratic." Wealth is more concentrated today than ever before in history, despite all the experiments that have taken place in socialism and social democracy. Political power can impose control over human beings, but it can't make capital function differently—that would take a fundamental social transformation. As long as the foundation of our economic system is *ownership,* capital will tend to accumulate into higher and higher concentrations, and the resulting inequalities will determine the dynamics of our society regardless of checks and balances.

Magnates

The market rewards skill, brilliance, and daring—but only to the extent that they produce profit.

The essential quality naturally selected for those at the top of the pyramid is that they make decisions on the basis of what concentrates the most power in their hands. That power doesn't come out of the air; it is comprised of others' capabilities and agency and effort.

They pass down all the costs of this accumulation of power that they can—not only to workers and consumers and victims of pollution, but also to their spouses and secretaries and housemaids. But they can't avoid the fact that they have to make decisions based on economic constraints or else lose their positions of power. Perhaps this is self-determination, but only inside a very narrow framework for what self-determination is.

You could say capitalism puts power in the worst hands, but that misses the point. It's not that the ones rewarded by the economy tend to be the worst people, but that—however selfish or generous they are—their positions are contingent on certain kinds of behavior. The moment an executive deprioritizes profit-making, he or his company is instantly replaced with a more ruthless contender. For example, in a world in which corporate decisions are governed by the necessity of producing good quarterly reports, CEOs are simply powerless to make decisions that place ecology over profit. They might promote ecological products or sustainable energy, but only as a marketing campaign or

PR move. Genuinely ecocentric decision-making can only occur outside the market.

So you don't have to believe all executives are bad people to conclude that capitalism itself is pernicious. On the contrary, the defenders of the free market are the ones who have to make arguments based on human nature. To excuse the destructiveness of the economy, they must argue that no other social system can motivate human beings and provide for their needs.

Who dies when they make a killing?

Politicians

Everybody hates politicians. This should be surprising, considering that their careers depend on being liked, but the reason is simple enough. They get their jobs by promising us the world, but their job is to keep it out of our hands—to *govern* it.

Like every other form of work, this governing imposes its own logic. Think about what goes on in the Pentagon and the Kremlin and the offices of every town hall. Those day-to-day activities are the same under Democrats as they are under Republicans; they're not much different in Moscow today than they were under Bolsheviks or even the Tsar. Politicians may wield power within the structures of the state, but those structures dictate what they can do with it.

To understand how this works, we have to begin in feudal Europe, when capitalism was just getting started and the fabric of society was simpler. Kings granted nobles power in return for military support; nobles gave vassals land in return for fealty; peasants and serfs gave their lords free labor and a share of what they produced in return for not being exterminated. Access to resources was determined by inherited status and an ever-shifting balance of allegiances. These hierarchies were explicit but extremely unstable: because there were few other ways to better one's lot, people were constantly rebelling and overturning them.

Eventually, however, monarchs began to consolidate power. To accomplish this, they had to construct what we know today as the apparatus of the state: they integrated their

henchmen into a single bureaucratic machine monopolizing military force, judicial legitimacy, and the regulation of commerce. Unlike the nobles of feudal times, the functionaries in this machine had specialized duties and limited authority; they answered directly to the monarchs who paid their wages, often with money borrowed from the banks that were springing up all over Europe.

The first politicians were ministers appointed by kings to operate this machinery. In some ways, they were bureaucrats like those under them; they had to be fairly competent in the fields they oversaw, like an attorney general or secretary of state today. But competence was often less important than the ability to curry favor with the king via flattery, bribes, or outlandish promises. This should sound familiar to anyone who follows contemporary politics.

Capitalism developed in a symbiotic relationship with the apparatus of the state. In feudal times, most people had obtained much of what they needed outside the exchange economy. But as the state consolidated power, the fields and pastures that had been held in common were privatized, and local minorities and overseas continents were ruthlessly plundered. As resources began to flow more dynamically, merchants and bankers gained increasing power and influence.

The North American and European revolutions of the 18th and 19th centuries brought an end to the reign of kings. Seeing the writing on the wall, merchants sided with the exploited and excluded. But the apparatus of the state was essential for protecting their wealth; so instead of abolishing the structures through which the king had ruled them, they argued that people should take them over and administer them "democratically." Consequently, "we the people" replaced the king as the sovereign power for politicians to court.

The state apparatus went on consolidating power independently of the individuals at its helm and the sovereign to whom they supposedly answered. Police, education, social services, militaries, financial institutions, and jurisprudence expanded and multiplied. In keeping with their symbiotic relationship with capitalism, all of these tended to produce docile workforces, stable markets, and a steady stream of resources. As they came to administer more and more aspects of society according to a body of specialized knowledge, it became ever more difficult to imagine life without them.

In the 20th century, a new wave of revolutions established the rule of this bureaucratic class throughout the "developing world." This time, merchants were often overthrown along with kings; but once again, the state apparatus itself was left intact, operated by a new generation of politicians who claimed to serve "the working class." Some called this "socialism," but properly speaking it was simply *state capitalism,* in which capital was controlled by government bureaucracy.

Today, capital and the state have almost completely replaced the hierarchies of the feudal era. Wealth and influence remain hereditary—hence the succession of Roosevelts and Bushes in the White House—but it is the structures themselves that dominate our lives rather than the individuals operating them. And while feudal hierarchies were fixed but fragile, these new structures are extremely resilient.

Some still hope that democracy will counteract the effects of capitalism. But it's no coincidence that the two spread across the world together: both preserve hierarchies while enabling maximum mobility within them. This channels discontent into internal competition, enabling individuals to change their positions without contesting the power imbalances built into society. The free market gives every sensible worker an incentive to remain invested in private ownership and competition; as long as it seems more feasible to better his own standing than to pull off a revolution, he'll choose competing for a promotion over class war. Similarly, democracy is the best way to maximize popular investment

A spectacle to distract

in the coercive institutions of the state because it gives the greatest possible number of people the feeling that they could have some influence over them.

In representative democracy as in capitalist competition, everyone supposedly gets a chance but only a few come out on top. If you didn't win, you must not have tried hard enough! This is the same rationalization used to justify the injustices of sexism and racism: look, you lazy bums, you could have been Bill Cosby or Hillary Clinton if you'd just *worked harder*. But there's not enough space at the top for all of us, no matter how hard we work.

When reality is generated via the media and media access is determined by wealth, elections are simply advertising campaigns. Market competition dictates which lobbyists gain the resources to determine the grounds upon which voters make their decisions. Under these circumstances, a political party is essentially a business offering investment opportunities in legislation. It's foolish to expect political representatives to oppose the interests of their clientele when they depend directly upon them for power.

But even if we could reform the electoral system and vote in representatives with hearts of gold, the state would still be an obstacle to consensual social structures and self-determination. Its essential function is to impose control: to *enforce*, to *punish*, to *administer*. In the absence of kings, domination continues—it's all the system is good for.

Modern debates between the political "left" and "right" generally center on how much control of capital should go to the state rather than to private enterprise. Both agree that power should be centralized in the hands of a professional elite; the only question is how this elite should be constituted. Leftists often argue their case by decrying the irrationality of the market and promising a more humane state of affairs.

Yet there's no evidence that we'd be better off if the state owned everything. From the Soviet Union to Nazi Germany, the 20th century offers plenty of examples of this, none of them promising. In view of their historical origins and the demands of maintaining power, it shouldn't be surprising that state bureaucracies are no better than corporate bureaucracies. All bureaucracy alienates human beings from their own potential, rendering it something external that they can only access through its channels.

While some politicians might oppose powerful individuals or classes, no politician will contest hierarchical power per se; like magnates, their position is contingent on the centralization of power, so they can do no different. In extreme cases, a government may replace one capitalist class with another—as the Bolsheviks did after the Russian Revolution—but no government will ever do away with private ownership, for governing necessarily entails controlling capital. If we want to create a world without work, we'll have to do so without politicians.

You will never ascend to the stage

Sometimes a candidate appears who says everything people have been saying to each other for a long time—he seems to have appeared from outside the world of politics, to really be *one of us*. By critiquing the system within its own logic, he subtly persuades people that it can be reformed—that it *could* work, if only the right people had power. Thus a lot of energy that might have gone into challenging the system itself is redirected into backing yet another candidate for office, who inevitably fails to deliver.

These candidates only receive so much attention because they draw on popular sentiments; the one thing they're good for is diverting energy from grass-roots movements. When they come to power and sell out the public, the opposition parties can capitalize on this to associate their supposedly radical ideas with the very problems they promised to solve—and channel disillusionment with government into yet another political campaign! So should we put our energy into supporting politicians, or into building the social momentum that forces them to take radical stances in the first place?

More frequently, we're terrorized into focusing on the electoral spectacle by the prospect of being ruled by the worst possible candidates. "What if *he* gets into power?" To think that things could get *even worse!*

But the problem is that politicians wield so much power in the first place—otherwise it wouldn't matter who held the reins. So long as this is the case, there will always be tyrants. This is why we have to put our energy into lasting solutions, not political campaigns.

Bosses

Who doesn't hate their boss? Even people who claim to like their bosses say so with a certain reserve: *he's not so bad . . . for a boss.*

Nobody likes being told what to do or turning a profit for someone else. These simple resentments keep things a little tense even without an anticapitalist movement. From the bosses' perspective, every day is a Kafkaesque struggle to cajole or coerce employees who would rather be anywhere else on earth. No one appreciates how tough it is at the top; everyone tells bosses what they want to hear, instead of the truth—not surprising, of course, considering the power differential. Small wonder the typical boss thinks the whole world would grind to a halt without bosses.

But workers hate bosses because bosses are *useless.* Bosses get in the way. The higher you rise in management, the less you're involved in practical day-to-day tasks and the less you know about them—hence the story of the incompetent worker who was promoted to ensure that he couldn't do any harm. In any case, most executives at the top of the corporate ladder did not start out at the bottom.

All this gives the lie to the narrative of meritocracy, the idea that people achieve money and power according to their skill and effort. Executives often make *hundreds of times* what their rank-and-file employees make; such dramatically unequal earnings cannot possibly reflect a real difference in how hard they work or how much they offer to the world. More pragmatic businessmen explain that these salaries are necessary to compete against other companies to recruit effective executives. But if these disparities seem inevitable, this only shows that the capitalist economy *cannot* reward people according to their actual contributions.

Ironically, it seems that the only way to escape bosses is to become one—that is, *to become what you hate*. Hence the ambivalence many workers display to career advancement.

BUT I WORKED HARD FOR MY MONEY! I PULLED MYSELF UP BY MY BOOTSTRAPS!

MAYBE YOU DID, BUT DON'T YOU THINK THE PEOPLE WHO CLEAN YOUR BATHROOMS WORK HARD, TOO? THERE SIMPLY ISN'T ENOUGH SPACE AT THE TOP FOR EVERYONE WHO WORKS HARD—AND I'M BETTING YOU DIDN'T START OUT CLEANING BATHROOMS.

BUT MY WEALTH CREATES JOBS FOR PEOPLE!

YOU THINK PEOPLE HAD NO WAY OF LIVING BEFORE YOU STARTED 'CREATING JOBS' FOR US? ON THE CONTRARY, IT *FORCES* JOBS ON US—WE USED TO BE *FREE*!

PICTURE THE BUSINESS OWNER of the old days: a shop-keeper, a family running a store, a small factory owner employing townspeople who walk to work. In all these cases, the owners were clearly identifiable, typically part of the same community as the workers.

When you hear about a company "going public," it sounds so collective and democratic: everyone can buy in and be part of the growth and success. But who's really accountable in this structure, and what kind of decisions does it produce?

I reflected on this during my decade as an employee of a Fortune 100 corporation. Publicly-traded corporations have owners, too, but you have to peel back many onion-like layers to learn anything about them. Technically, every shareholder is an owner with legal rights to a share of the firm. But the total number of shares in a company often extends to hundreds of millions; it would take diligent research to learn anything about everyone involved.

Visible individual investors are rare, though there's still an occasional wealthy family or trust with holdings big enough to warrant special treatment. More often, share ownership is divided among institutional investors: hedge funds, holding companies, private corporations, evil investment firms—think Goldman Sachs—and the real *dark matter* of the economy, mutual fund participants. The last group includes everyone with a 401K, union-managed retirement fund, or individual retirement account. Fifty years ago, safe-deposit boxes held fancy stock certificates from a short list of companies: "We found a certificate for 100 shares of IBM after he died." Now a wide range of people each own tiny pieces of hundreds of companies, and those holdings change daily.

The net effect at the corporate decision-making level is that executives have free rein to invoke the mantra of "shareholder value" with little risk of actual shareholder feedback. Since the shareholders change constantly, focusing on shareholder value doesn't mean answering to actual individuals who might have scruples of some kind. Rather, it means doing whatever it takes to make the company profitable and thus attractive to hypothetical investors. All the "ancillary criteria"—environmental impact, effects on employees and even customers—become secondary to what contributes to the value of each shareholder's stocks.

What I observed at the micro-level was that whenever managers and executives wrestled with emotionally-loaded decisions, they fell back on shareholder value to resolve the dilemma. The investors were an abstract entity that could justify anything; even if there were real people somewhere on the other end of those shares, we could only picture them as a sort of personified profit motive.

Meetings followed a familiar pattern. We dialed into the conference line and exchanged pleasantries with colleagues in other parts of the country—weather, sports, purchases, travel-related conversation—until a critical mass of participants joined the video conference. Aside from the occasional executive support person, everyone on the call earned $250K to $850K a year. Most were married and childless; the few with school-age kids had stay-at-home partners and nanny support. They sent their children to private college-prep schools and exercised at country clubs. I'd look around at them and reflect on how their decisions affected so many families of less means.

I remember one in-person all-day session that ran behind schedule; at five p.m. the group discussed whether to continue into the evening or schedule additional time the following day. One vice president, a divorced father of three in his late forties, mentioned he'd need to get home to make dinner for his kids, ages seven, ten, and twelve. Genuinely thinking she was being helpful, the senior vice president suggested, "Can't you just have a pizza delivered?"

Another phenomenon I noticed was that the further up the organizational hierarchy a person rose, the more and more limited the things he could do to effect change became. The most basic limitation concerned direct human interaction. When you go from directing a group of ten people to directing a hundred and then a thousand, it becomes impossible to have meaningful contact with everyone. You end up doing "road shows" or town hall meetings, and rely more and more on email messages to influence individuals.

The one big move you can make at that level is the classic corporate reorganization. Structural rearrangements are often accompanied by job eliminations, which not only save the company money but also create chaos and divert attention. One CIO I worked for, when asked about a reorganization that would return the structure to what it had been six years earlier, explained, "It's like when you clean out a closet. You take everything out, you put almost everything back, but because you've rearranged things, it gives you a chance to see it differently. The particular structure you use ends up being less important than the fact that you gave everyone a way of seeing things differently."

Ironically, this leader was actually very well liked, in part for a decision he made in his first few weeks. As the first step in downsizing, he eliminated the entire managerial layer immediately below him. The select few that had clawed their way within a step of the top were all let go. No one felt sorry for them—they all got golden parachutes—and it endeared him to everyone further below. He benefited from that goodwill over the next three years as he relocated or laid off another 30 percent of the workforce.

All this hints at the cognitive dissonance in managers' attitudes to their employees. They love them, nurture them, and reward them—scheming all the while to get rid of their positions.

What motivated these leaders? How did they sleep at night? The simple answer is that they were true believers in capitalism. "When we raise the water level, all boats rise"—they embraced this idea to justify the flow of money to the wealthy. They subscribed to trickle-down theories and just about any practice that kept money flowing, especially up and laterally. Their own life experiences reinforced those beliefs. The workers in their organizations often felt the same way, or hoped to. Only when the economy entered free fall did some of my colleagues entertain questions about the system itself; even then, their range of thought remained myopic.

I remember when one vice president sent a note to her organization of about 350 technical support employees. Her message was meant to reassure workers fearing for their jobs as waves of downsizings loomed. She explained how, in her career, she always did certain things to prepare just in case her own job was eliminated—things like paying off her credit cards, selling her vacation homes, and the like. She was married with no children; she'd recently bragged about spending thousands of dollars for one of Bon Jovi's guitars during a trip to the East Coast. Her recommendation that workers "prepare financially and emotionally" resonated the way you might expect.

Ironically, after years of helping execute corporate down-sizings and relocating employees' jobs to less expensive locales, I was finally made redundant myself during the 2008 crisis. I knew all about the process—it had been my job to explain company policy to those we were letting go—but I was surprised what a gut shock it was to be on the other side of it: "We're not getting rid of everyone, but we're getting rid of *you.*"

For years I'd thought about working for a non-profit company, but the crisis was the worst time to be cut loose. There weren't any jobs available, and the higher your salary is the longer it takes to find a new position. At long last I landed a job with a non-profit healthcare provider.

It didn't turn out to be much different from the for-profit sector. In fact, they were hiring a lot of people from the finance industry—professionals like me who had overseen the streamlining of our corporations and then been downsized ourselves—so they could become more competitive. Now they're restructuring and dismissing employees, too.

A few weeks ago I was in the elevator with a manager who has worked there for years. She was practically giddy about the layoffs: she said they'd make the non-profit more efficient, which would enable it to fulfill its mission statement more effectively. Here it was again, the mantra of shareholder value in a new form. As long as organizations serve abstract ends rather than flesh-and-blood people, it doesn't matter whether those abstractions represent stockholders, customers, or even the common good.

Superstars

Why do we love Lady Gaga—not just the catchy hooks, but the costumes, the rumors, the *mythology*? Why are we fascinated by romantic comedies and talk shows even when they insult our intelligence and contradict our politics? Why do the lives of famous strangers seem so much more *real* than our own lives?

Perhaps we're drawn to them because they embody *our* creativity—the creative potential of all the exploited—purchased from us, concentrated, and sold back. Bruce Springsteen would be just another singer-songwriter without the vocal trainers and production engineers, the technicians who work the lights, and the adoring gaze of millions; together these produce most of the meaning we find in him, as well as the illusion that he is solely responsible for it. Because human beings are social animals, attention *creates* meaning and thus value: when everyone else runs to see what's going on, each of us can't help but do the same.

Thus the collective creativity and potential of a whole society is channeled into a few figureheads. Of course we love them, or at least love to hate them—they represent the only way to access *our own* displaced potential.

The same goes for blockbusters like *Fight Club* and *Avatar* that epitomize the alienation they critique. Stories that once were told around the fire now circulate through the market, including the stories that criticize it. Now even when we sit around a fire we talk about episodes from movies and television! Whenever we turn on a movie rather than generating our own stories and culture, we are selling ourselves short—not so much by being spectators as by consenting to access the storytelling part of ourselves only through the mediation of the economy.

Can we escape this by making our own media, forming audiences without superstars? The more people invest meaning in their own lives and social circles, the more powerful and capable they are likely to be: consider the role that counterculture has often played in resistance movements. But in the age of mass communication, the affairs of any small milieu can feel insignificant by comparison; reality is comprised of *everyone's* points of reference, not just the ones we choose subculturally. Meanwhile, focusing on *representations* of ourselves and each other can produce the same alienation as focusing on the images of strangers.

In a media-centered society, attention is a currency alongside other currencies. It functions as a kind of capital: the more you have, the easier it is to accrue, and after a certain point it seems to flow to you almost automatically. In some venues, the pursuit of *attention itself* has nearly superseded other forms of economic competition—think of graffiti tagging and internet memes. But the attention available on the market is qualitatively different from the attention friends and lovers lavish on one another. Even the most famous stars can't derive that kind of nourishment from their fame; if their high casualty rate is any indication, fame is an *obstacle* to healthy relationships. In this regard, stardom mirrors other forms of success in which a few people accumulate substitutes for what *everyone* has lost.

New decentralized technologies offer almost everybody the chance to be microstars: to propagate images of ourselves in a world in which no one really has time to focus on anyone else in person. Rather than redressing the effects of unequal distribution of attention, this renders everyone equally small and alone. The alienation generated by the existence of superstars doesn't diminish with the coronation of more stars; it increases.

Professionals

What do lawyers, accountants, administrators, professors, and doctors all have in common? *Expertise.*

There's nothing bad about knowing how to do things. But expertise is distinct from mere proficiency. It connotes privileged access to a sphere of knowledge others can only approach through an intermediary.

Of course, plenty of people are at the mercy of auto mechanics when it comes to repairing their cars. The difference is that you can teach yourself to fix cars, and no one can stop you from fixing your own car—but you can't just read some books and set up shop as a professor. Mechanics, carpenters, plumbers, and other tradesmen are subject to some of the same controls as engineers and pharmacists, but the further up the pyramid you go the more strict and exclusive those controls are.

Expertise is constructed by institutions that regulate and license those who practice a profession, legitimizing them as *professionals*. This excludes amateurs and people who learned their skills in other frameworks. Such exclusion enforces quality standards, discouraging snake oil salesmen pursuing the incentives of free enterprise. But it also ensures that certain skills remain the private domain of powerful organizations, intensifying the divide between these *authorities* and everyone else.

This division elevates professionals as a class, assuring them power, prestige, high income, and more autonomy than most workers. It isn't surprising that professional associations use their influence to protect these privileges and discipline anyone who threatens them, including dissidents within their own ranks. This also guarantees certain educational institutions a monopoly on the market of aspiring professionals.

In contrast to the practical skills associated with less prestigious trades, *expertise* often refers to spheres that are entirely socially constructed. One cannot be a bishop or a lawyer without the validation of the Church or judiciary. Professionalization keeps common people at a distance from aspects of their own society: rather than developing a personal practice of faith or justice, they must rely on experts.

The effects of this specialization extend to our relationships with our own bodies. Once upon a time, healing was practiced by and accessible to the poor. One of the major effects of the witch-hunts of the 14th through 17th centuries was to suppress this popular art; over the following centuries, similar campaigns concentrated medical knowledge and authority in fewer and fewer hands, opening the way for medicine to become a monolithic male-dominated profession. Today our own bodies appear unfamiliar to us, enabling the health care and insurance industries to make a killing keeping us alive.

In fields that were professionalized more recently, it's still easy to see how this has imposed a hierarchical framework on previously grass-roots pursuits. For example, as the movements against domestic violence and sexual assault sought funding from foundations and government agencies, they were transformed into service-providing organizations that demanded proper credentials of their employees. Today the authors of the manuals used by some of these organizations wouldn't qualify for jobs in them.

Professionalization privatizes skills and innovations that once circulated freely, making it impossible to access them except through the economy. It is one of the ways that capitalism centralizes know-how and legitimacy as well as wealth.

Exclusivity is our business.

Middle Management

The middle manager is simultaneously a laborer and a representative of the capitalist class. She is forced to behave like an executive without the same rewards.

Like the employees below her, she has to implement decisions made without her input—and when she does well, the credit goes to the ones who give her orders. Like the executives above her, she cannot simply sell hours of her life but must *become* her job, taking her work home with her. It's her responsibility to implement corporate policies, motivate employees, and maintain day-to-day discipline and control. Everyone in middle management hopes to advance quickly to a higher position—but the higher you go in the pyramid, the fewer positions there are.

A few decades ago, when employees might work for the same corporation their entire lives, middle management positions seemed like a step in a slow, steady process of advancement. That dream came to an end in the 1980s, when technological advancements enabled corporations to "downsize" middle managers by the thousand. Yet middle management remains, both as a specific role in the economy and as an existential condition afflicting all but those at the very top and bottom of the pyramid. The ones above us manage us, we manage the ones below us—but how long can *we* manage, ourselves?

"
In the shift from manual skills to the art of selling and servicing people, personal traits of employees are drawn into the sphere of exchange and become commodities in the labor market. Kindness and friendliness become aspects of personalized service or of public relations of big firms, rationalized to further sales. With anonymous insincerity, the successful person thus makes an instrument of his own appearance and personality.

Sincerity is detrimental to one's job, until the rules of salesmanship and business become a "genuine" aspect of oneself. Tact is a series of little lies about one's feelings, until one is emptied of such feelings.

The personality market, the most decisive effect and symptom of the great salesroom, underlies the all-pervasive distrust and alienation characteristic of metropolitan people. Without common values and mutual trust, the cash nexus that links one man to another in transient contact has been made subtle in a dozen ways and come to bite deeper into all areas of life.

People are required to pretend interest in others in order to manipulate them. In the course of time, as this ethic spreads, one learns that manipulation is inherent in every human contact. Men are estranged from one another as each secretly tries to make an instrument of the other, and in time a full circle is made: one makes an instrument of himself, and is estranged from it as well.

> – C. Wright Mills
> *White Collar: The American Middle Classes*, 1951

Self-Employment

"Self-employed" describes a wide range of positions—from tutors and babysitters to proprietors of mom-and-pop stores, from the flower vendors on the street corner to the successful artists of the "creative class." Self-employment is associated with personal freedom; but managing your own business generally makes more demands on your time than working for a corporation, and not necessarily at comparable rates.

If the problem with capitalism is that bosses don't pay workers the full value of their labor, self-employment seems like the solution: if everyone were self-employed, wouldn't that mean nobody could be exploited? But exploitation isn't just a matter of having a boss—it's the result of uneven distribution of *capital*. If all you have for capital is an ice-cream stand, you're not going to accumulate profit at the same rate as the landlord who owns your apartment building, even if both of you are sole proprietors. The patterns that concentrate capital in fewer and fewer hands can play out as easily *between* business entities as *within* them.

So self-employment is not the same as self-determination. Self-employment gives you more *agency* without offering any more *liberty:* you get to manage your own affairs, but only on the market's terms. Being self-employed simply means organizing the sale of your labor yourself and personally taking on all the risks of competing. Imagine how many corporations have made a pretty penny selling goods and services to aspiring entrepreneurs that quickly went out of business and returned to wage labor.

Like the magnate in miniature, the self-employed worker survives and acquires resources to the precise extent to which she turns a profit. More so than the wage laborer, she has to internalize the logic of the market, taking its pressures and values to heart. The entrepreneur learns to examine everything from her time to her personal relationships in terms of market value. She comes to see herself the way a timber company looks at a forest; each entrepreneur is at once boss and bossed, her very psyche split into capitalist and exploited facets. In the end, it's more efficient for workers to supervise their own integration into the market than for corporations or governments to impose it on them.

Accordingly, today we're seeing a shift from the paradigm of worker-as-employee to worker-as-entrepreneur: rather than simply obeying instructions and taking home a paycheck, even workers who aren't self-employed are encouraged to *invest themselves* in the same manner. Progressive teachers try to engage their students as "active learners" instead of simply indoctrinating them; commanders devolve tactical decision-making to individual units whose training emphasizes "combat readiness" over mere willingness to carry out orders. As jobs become more precarious, work experience becomes an investment aimed at securing future employment—your résumé is as important as your wages. The last self-employed artisans of the old days are dying out, but the entrepreneur might be the model citizen of a world order still under construction. The old-fashioned narrative of independence and self-reliance is absurd when both have become impossible: rather than cultivating independence, the point of modern self-management is to incorporate each individual seamlessly into the economy.

Despite these developments, some still consider locally-owned businesses an alternative to corporate capitalism.

It's naïve to imagine small businesses are somehow more accountable to their communities: business ventures of all kinds succeed or fail according to their success extracting profit *from* communities. Small businesses might gain loyal customers by being a little less predatory, but only to the extent that this succeeds as *advertising,* and only insofar as consumers can afford to pay extra for this luxury. In the world of business, "social responsibility" is either a marketing strategy or a handicap. The dichotomy between local businesses and multinationals only serves to redirect those frustrated with capitalism into supporting small-scale capitalists, legitimizing ventures that ultimately will either accumulate capital at others' expense or be supplanted by more merciless contenders.

Countless societies have existed that didn't believe in private ownership of capital, but no historian has ever documented a society in which capital was evenly distributed among a population of self-employed businessmen. Such a thing could only last as long as it took for some of the businessmen to start profiting off the rest. Relying on small businesses to solve the problems generated by capitalism is less realistic than attempting to bring about the end of capitalism itself.

Factories

The factories that produce most of the goods we think of as necessities today emerged at the end of the 18th century with the onset of the Industrial Revolution. This transformed manufacturing, agriculture, transportation, and almost every other aspect of life.

From the very beginning, mechanization sparked resistance. Several centuries of agricultural privatization had already driven most peasants off their land, and now new technologies were reducing skilled craftsmen to beggars. The stinking, noisy factory towns must have seemed like a scene from hell itself, sucking in the dispossessed and constructing an infernal machine from their bodies. In response, the Luddites burned mills and machinery, posing such a threat that at one point more British troops were deployed to fight them than were ranged against Napoleon.

The factory system was a mixed blessing for the capitalists who created it. On the one hand, it consolidated their power as the owning class: artisans working at home with their own tools simply couldn't compete. This enabled capitalists to control workers' activity directly, whereas before they could only buy the products of labor. Moreover, industrialization gave the capitalists of a few nations a tremendous advantage over their competitors abroad, setting the stage for a brutal new wave of European colonization.

On the other hand, mechanization required an unprecedented concentration of workers, both in the factories themselves and in the urban centers where factories were located. This concentration could have explosive results, as it did in 1871 when workers and poor urbanites rose in rebellion against the French government to establish the short-lived Paris Commune. Even between such upheavals, capitalists were vulnerable to strikes, and they never knew when a workplace disturbance might explode into an insurrection.

Factory owners had another problem, too. They could produce more goods than ever before, but they were reaching the limits of market: there simply weren't enough wealthy people to buy everything they could produce. Since every hour of labor made them a profit, employers compelled the downtrodden populace to work as much as possible. But as resistance grew and returns dwindled, capitalists had to find a new way to maximize profits. Instead of trying to squeeze even more hours of labor from employees, they set out to squeeze more production out of every labor hour. Using the unprecedented powers of supervision that the factory gave them, they reorganized the work process to make it ever more efficient and intensive.

In the early 20th century, automobile magnate Henry Ford hit on the winning combination of assembly lines, standardization, and cheap products, inaugurating the era of mass production and consumption. Ford looked at the factory itself as a machine and set out to make workers into more efficient cogs in it. This made tasks increasingly specialized and repetitive, so workers had less and less of a sense of the total context of their labor. Over the next few decades, as mass production and mass consumption became the norm worldwide, this alienation came to be mirrored in society at large, which became a sort of social factory operating according to the logic of the assembly line. Schools mass-produced interchangeable workers ready to take up posts anywhere; automobiles inscribed new channels of commerce on the landscape in the form of highways and suburbs.

Of course, worker populations were still dangerously concentrated, and this intensification of work had the potential to spark an intensification of resistance. The use of automation made it difficult to foster competition on the shop floor the way Ford's predecessors had. Worse, workers were so averse to the mind-numbing experience of the assembly line that they kept quitting in droves; Ford was losing money constantly training new replacements.

His solution was to buy off the workforce as a whole by giving his employees a share in industrial prosperity. Starting in 1914, Ford paid his factory workers twice the going rate, granted them eight-hour workdays, and offered them a profit-sharing plan so they could buy the same Model Ts they produced. The resulting expansion of the market for automobiles enabled Ford to absorb the cost of high wages by increasing production and sales year after year. This compromise was soon taken up across the industrialized world; in effect, this marked the invention of the modern middle class, along with modern leisure time. Capitalists had made virtue of necessity; forced to grant money and free time to the exploited, they invented mass consumption so the money and time they conceded would eventually come back to them.

Raising wages helped Ford thwart an attempt to unionize his factory. But in the long run, one result of his compromise was that unions, long the outlaw opposition to capitalism, finally found an essential role in its functioning. By forcing employers to keep wages high enough that workers could afford consumer goods, they kept capitalists from destroying their own consumer base. By focusing on the wage contract, unions channeled worker struggles away from outright revolution into institutionalized collective bargaining. Union bureaucracies arose alongside corporate bureaucracies, staffed by professionals whose chief interest was advancing their careers. Unions ceased to oppose the intensification and expansion of work itself—what was good for *work* was good for unions, whether or not it was good for workers.

This professionalization of labor struggle took place in "developing countries" as well, transforming struggles against work into struggles for a greater share of what it produced. Ironically, wherever the capitalist class had not developed enough to implement Ford's innovations, these were imposed by the bureaucratic representatives of labor struggle. In Soviet Russia, for example, "Fordism" was embraced as a model for speedy industrialization. Josef Stalin proclaimed approvingly that "American efficiency is that indomitable force which neither knows nor recognizes obstacles" as he presided over a brutal transition to mechanized agriculture at the cost of millions of lives. It's possible to see the Bolshevik revolution as an exotic version of the Fordist compromise, in which workers' struggles were channeled into support-ing a new bureaucratic ruling class in return for a share of consumer goods.

In any case, compromises within capitalism rarely last long. Starting in the 1960s, capitalists faced a new round of crises as their strategies for economic expansion once again reached their limits and a new generation of work-ers broke with the unions to rebel against work. The youth movements that shook the globe from Paris and Prague to Chicago and Shanghai often framed their project in utopian terms, but they were revolting against something concrete and familiar: their parents' truce with exploitation. The costs of this truce were becoming apparent in the destruction of the natural world and the alienation of daily life. At the same time, the industries that had benefited most from the Fordist compromise—the ones manufacturing automobiles, household appliances, and other durable goods—were begin-ning to decline as they found fewer and fewer new buyers for their products.

And so, like Ford before them, capitalists reorganized the processes of production and consumption to make them stabler and more profitable. Aided by new communication technologies, they spread manufacturing out across the entire planet, sidestepping unionized or rebellious workforces and exploiting whoever was most desperate. Employers scaled back formal long-term employment in favor of more flexible forms of labor, in order to unload the risks of the market directly on workers. Economies of scale, in which corporations saved money by mass-producing a few standardized commodities, were supplemented by economies of scope, in which the same infrastructure was used to produce a wide array of items. Consumer markets diversified accordingly, and the mass-produced individual—a conformist who had nonetheless posed a real threat to public order in times of upheaval—was replaced by an infinite range of different consumer identities. Thus the labor force that had been so dangerous when it was united became fragmented in every way.

Once again, these changes in production and consumption were inscribed upon society and the earth. In the US, the social factory no longer produces workers who intend to invest their whole lives in one career; the booming industrial cities of the previous century have become a desolate Rust Belt dotted with cafés and universities.

Today there are still factories, but computerized equipment and data-processing enable them to employ fewer and fewer workers. The increasingly superfluous workforce has been absorbed by the service sector in wealthy parts of the world; in poor countries, it is left to fend for itself. Just as Ford modeled the factory on the machine, the assembly line provides the model for global supply chains, networks of large and small manufacturers contracted and coordinated by giant corporations: raw materials can be made in India and Brazil, assembled in Hong Kong, and sold in Los Angeles.

Unlike the factories of old, these networks aren't vulnerable to the dangers posed by a concentrated workforce; if one node of this vast assembly line becomes rebellious, its role can be transferred to another node as far away as the opposite side of the globe.

Paradoxically, this "post-Fordist" economy revives forms of labor that seemed to disappear with the ascendance of automation. Since major industries no longer need most of the people that capitalism has dispossessed, workers can be had for cheap in sweatshops around the world—low-tech, miserable workplaces that require little investment in specialized machinery. Such sweatshops are ideally suited to the fluid demands of contemporary production, which might require sneaker stitching one day and T-shirt sleeves the next. They are often the only way to meet the demands of a consumer market based on the novelty and uniqueness of a million different products.

In this context, unions are woefully outflanked and outmoded. Institutionalized regulation of wage labor no longer seems necessary to stabilize the market, so their usefulness for capitalism has ended; production no longer depends on the rigid demographic concentrations that once made them such a threat to business, either. Anticapitalists are still casting around for new forms of resistance that could take the place of the union and the strike.

ra·tion·al·ize (răsh′ə-nə-līz′) *v. –tr.* **1.** Attempt to explain or justify (one's own or another's behavior or attitude) with logical, plausible reasons, even if these are not true or appropriate: *she couldn't rationalize her urge to return to the cottage.* See note at LIE. **2.** Make (a company, process, or industry) more efficient by reorganizing it in such a way as to dispense with unnecessary personnel or equipment: *his success was due primarily to his ability to rationalize production.*

Teachers and Students

Anyone who has spent time with small children knows how much they love to learn. From the very beginning, they imitate everyone around them. Without this instinct enabling every new generation to pick up the knowledge and skills of the previous ones, our species would have gone extinct long ago.

It takes a lot to beat this natural curiosity out of children. You have to take them away from their families, isolate them in sterile environments with only a few overworked adults, and teach them that learning is a *discipline*. You have to send them to school.

It wasn't until the 19ᵗʰ century that mass education came into its own in Europe. The family, the oldest socializing institution, no longer sufficed to prepare children for their roles in a changing society—especially with working families increasingly fragmented by the industrial revolution. Once limits were put on child labor, kids had to spend the day *somewhere*. Governments saw compulsory schooling as a way to produce a docile population: obedient soldiers for the army, compliant laborers for industry, dutiful clerks and civil servants. Social reformers saw it differently, as a way to uplift humanity—but it was the governments who got to implement it.

Compulsory education spread alongside industrialization, and eventually education became an industry in its own right. The state-managed incarnation of the industry still functions to keep young people off the streets and program them with standardized curricula. The private incarnation has become a profitable sector of the economy: abstracted out of daily life, education is a commodity to be bought and sold like any other.

In a mechanized world, in which self-checkout at the grocery store and electronic check-in at the airport are replacing the jobs that used to keep citizens integrated into society, what can be done with all the surplus workers? One solution is to postpone their entry into the workforce. Today's aspiring employee spends more time than ever before studying to gain an advantage, a longer list of credentials, another selling point on her résumé. This helps send the message that the misfortunes of the unemployed and unsuccessful are their own fault—they should have gotten more education.

When power was chiefly hereditary, only the wealthy and powerful sent their children to school. In the current credit-based economy, in which many workers live beyond their means in hopes of bettering themselves, it's much easier to aspire to wealth and power—for a price. If you want a decent job, you have to pay thousands or tens of thousands for the prerequisite degrees. This traps students in decades of debt, forcing them to sell themselves wherever the market will take them—a sophisticated form of indentured servitude. The more overeducated the work force, the pickier employers become; and in a volatile economy, workers have to return to school again and again.

Today degrees are openly discussed as investments in capital. A degree is worth a certain amount of potential future income, and some degrees are more valuable than others. Now there's talk of decreasing student loans to students seeking degrees in less profitable fields such as the humanities. This follows the logic of the market, since the ones who receive those degrees are less likely to be able to repay loans—even if those fields of study can improve human life in ways that defy financial calibration. Meanwhile, austerity measures are cutting away the last vestiges of the university as an oasis of learning for its own sake.

Of course, millions of young people have no hope of going to college. Early in life, children are put on one of two education tracks according to social class; these can take the form of private and public schools, suburban and inner city schools, or classes for "advanced" students alongside classes for *everyone else*. For the majority foreordained to fail, the school system is a gigantic holding tank; the ones who rebel are shuttled directly from detention to prison. Many schools now resemble prisons, with police officers, metal detectors, and other mechanisms to normalize authoritarian control from an early age.

Despite the glut of college graduates on the market, some liberals still maintain that the solution to poverty and other problems is more education. But the further up the pyramid you go the fewer positions there are; no amount of public education can change this. At best, graduates from disadvantaged backgrounds might replace those in privileged positions, but for every person who climbs the social ladder someone else has to descend it. Usually, more education just means more debt.

Another liberal precept is the notion of academia as *the marketplace of ideas.* The marketplace metaphor is apt enough: like human beings, ideas have to compete on the uneven terrain of capitalism. Some are backed by chancellors and media moguls, dollars by the million or billion, entire military-industrial complexes; others are literally born in prison. Despite this, the ones that rise to the top are bound to be the best—just as the most successful businessmen must be superior to everyone else. According to this school of thought, capitalism persists because everyone from billionaire to bellboy agrees it is the best *idea.*

WE TEACH
YOU WORK
THEY PROFIT

But students don't develop their ideas in a vacuum; their conclusions are bound to be influenced by their class interests. The further you advance in the education system, the wealthier the student body is likely to be, especially with tuition rising while government grants decline. Consequently, reactionary ideas tend to accumulate academic prestige. If some conservatives still regard universities as hotbeds of radicalism, this is simply because the class interests of professors are not as reactionary as those of executives.

This isn't to say that wealthy children are born looking out for number one. It takes at least as much social engineering to produce entitled managers as it does to produce subservient employees. Most of this occurs subtly. For example, the curriculum for honors students includes nothing about how to grow or prepare food, make or mend clothing, or repair engines; the implication is that if these students do well, there will always be poor people to do these things for them. Thus the education that prepares them to hold power simultaneously incapacitates them when it comes to meeting their basic needs outside the economy, making any alternative appear genuinely life-threatening.

Though teachers are on the front lines imposing discipline on the poor and legitimizing the privileges of the rich, they're not really to blame. Lots of teachers are terrific people. Some can be great mentors or friends outside the constraints of school. Many have given up the chance to make more money because they believe teaching is important even though it pays poorly. But by and large the roles they are forced to play in the classroom prevent them from making the most of their gifts and their desire to do right by the next generation. Here as elsewhere, the system is powered by those who think they can reform it.

The Service Industry

Two centuries ago the majority of US workers were employed extracting resources directly from the earth—farming, fishing, and mining. The industrial revolution drew much of this workforce into manufacturing. Since then, technological progress has continuously reduced the need for labor in both agriculture and manufacturing, while factories have moved overseas for cheaper workforces. So it is that today the vast majority of US laborers create services rather than material goods.

The standardization and mechanization that Ford brought to the factory appeared in the service sector a generation later. Corporate franchises like Walmart and McDonald's industrialized the consumer end of the market, transforming the social terrain with mass-produced branding and publicity; meanwhile, call centers introduced the assembly line model into personal services. Small businesses that had served the same markets as these giants simply couldn't compete. The next generation of small businesses had to focus on providing specialized luxuries rather than staples: health food stores, vintage boutiques, underground entertainment venues. This corresponded to the diversification of consumer goods that followed the economic crises of the 1970s: just as the models for production had shifted from artisans' workshops to factories to sweatshops, consumption shifted from mom-and-pop stores to corporate chains supplemented by independent shops.

Today the service sector includes a vast range of occupations. At one end are white-collar jobs like sales and programming that have more in common with management than with the traditional activities of the exploited. At the other end are fast-food restaurants and call centers, which only differ from factories in that they accumulate nothing regardless of how hard they work their employees.

These extremes are starting to resemble each other. High-end jobs such as teaching are increasingly subject to corporate standardization, which replaces the individual skills traditionally associated with professional labor with impersonal procedures and protocols anyone can follow. Meanwhile, industries like food service increasingly demand the appearance of expertise—we have to be hiking consultants, baristas, or "sandwich professionals" just to hold a part-time job. Across the entire service sector, capitalists require the same thing: *flexible conformity*. There's no more room for "I'm new here" than there is for "I know how to do my damn job."

Technological progress replaces services with goods the same way it replaces manufacturing jobs with machines. A few generations ago the wealthy hired maids to wash their dishes, but today most households are equipped with a mechanical dishwasher. So while labor-saving innovations have shifted the bulk of the economy into the service sector, the service jobs that remain are the ones that haven't been easy to turn into goods—or the ones for which workers can be bought cheaper than machines.

Consequently, the transition from manufacturing economy to service economy corresponded with the entry of more women into the workplace. Women were typically paid lower wages, so they could compete better against machines for jobs. There are parts of the world where a male-dominated manufacturing sector has been almost entirely replaced by a female-dominated service sector. In the US, the shift from

HANG IN THERE

single-income to dual-income households helped mask the general decline in wages.

But why would *more* workers enter the economy just as manufacturing jobs were being eliminated? And how can capitalists turn a profit from labor that produces nothing?

Let's not be misled by our own experience: at least as much money is being made in manufacturing today as fifty or a hundred years ago. The difference is that technology has rendered most of us obsolete. Since fewer workers are needed to produce material goods, more people end up looking for work, and this drives down wages. When wages are low, it's cheaper for capitalists to hire employees who do nothing but promote their products; and since their competitors can do the same thing, they're forced to do so to stay competitive. This applies not only to sales representatives but also to the smiling face in the shoe store, the friendly voice on the tech support line, the obliging local at the tourist destination, the paper-pusher at the Better Business Bureau.

This explains why so much of the service industry focuses on creating ambiences conducive to consumer spending: hotels, cafés, restaurants, casinos, marketing and advertising. Customer service is becoming more central to the economy than merchandise; corporations don't just sell *things,* but also attention, hospitality, empathy, assistance, *interaction*—everything that used to be a free part of social life. The service industry is the thin layer of living flesh stretched over the iron machinery of the economy, stoking the engines of desire that drive it.

If capitalism were simply a way to meet material needs, it would make no sense that people work harder now that less labor is required for production. But capitalism isn't just a way to meet material needs; it's a social system based in alienated relationships. As long as the economy distributes access to resources according to wealth, advances in manufacturing technology will simply force workers to seek other livelihoods. The machine no longer needs us, but it still needs us to keep working.

Fortunately for capitalists, organizing against work is even harder in the service sector than it was in the factory. Like sweatshop workers, service workers are spread out across thousands of individual workplaces with little opportunity to forge ties or conspire together, and acts of resistance can easily be suppressed or concealed. In addition, when employees and employment both tend to be transient, workers have little leverage or incentive to resist.

Other obstacles arise from within. Despite the ways service jobs often resemble each other, many service workers don't see themselves as part of an exploited class. Because their work often involves some management duties, it's easier

We wash your dishes and hate your guts

for them to identify with the perspective of management regardless of whether they like their actual bosses. In some ways, identifying with one's job has always been a part of the service industry: *hello, my name is Pierre and I'll be your waiter for the evening.* Paying salaries in part via tips, for example, is a way to turn workers into little entrepreneurs who have to market themselves directly to customers. In today's competitive and unpredictable market, even the temp-worker has to see himself as a sort of entrepreneur.

Service workers who refuse to identify with their jobs often do so in the name of a "true calling" that they pursue outside of work hours with this same enterprising spirit. As art, adventure, and social life are all absorbed into the logic of productive investment, it becomes easy to look at your time at work as a capital outlay that enables you to pursue your dreams off the clock, like a new business owner paying rent on her storefront in hopes of future success. The flexible, temporary nature of service employment encourages this attitude; if additional free time is "more valuable" than extra wages, we have the freedom to work less, and if not, we can try to work more. In this way, the mentality of self-employment is extended to individuals who might otherwise contest employment itself.

Seen in this light, the victories of specialized small businesses over corporate giants in the service sector may indicate a new phase in the economic absorption of the individual. The special innovation of the new boutiques is that, in contrast to Walmart and McDonald's, it is their unique and irreducible qualities that sell them. A worker's personal quirks and secrets, previously the only territory beyond the reach of the market, become commodities to be sold like any other. In this regard, the service industry represents a front in the total colonization of our social lives.

I KNEW FROM AGE FOUR that I wanted to be a cartoonist. After watching Commander Mark on public access, I thought I'd work for Disney or some other giant media conglomerate. I would be richer than my father, and his before him—not really famous or anything, but successful enough.

I held on to this idea for quite a while. I didn't realize until I was already well into my service-industry career that my little American dream was no longer possible by the time I was old enough to live it out. Technological advances and sweatshop labor had done away with the central role of the cartoonist in producing animated series. So because I loved coffee I ended up working in a café, and because our band needed posters I began to teach myself graphic design. This is still how I make a living.

I've been fired from a lot of jobs. K-mart, Whole Foods, some smoothie place, and a whole lot of cafés. I usually tell potential employers that I left my previous job to travel or for another business venture—being a "freelance graphic designer" makes a good excuse, and bosses love it when you're a "self-motivated entrepreneur." Over time, I realized $6.50 to $8.00 an hour is only going to change with inflation. But despite having some talent and knowing how to talk about typography and layout, I have no idea how to compete for real design work, so I don't think I'm gonna get out of the service sector any time soon.

At some point I came to terms with this and set out to improve my lot by other means. Since there are no unions in my industry—especially not in independent cafés—we have to develop our own means of asserting our interests. This started out with petty theft and small acts of sabotage at work, but it also tied in with going to punk shows and protests against globalization and the war. I enjoyed the confrontations with police and the feeling of asserting ourselves collectively—but I couldn't figure out how to bring that to my workplace, which was still the place I spent most of my time.

At the next café I worked at, we figured out that the monthly store meeting with the bosses was purely symbolic and called our own meeting. Eight of the twelve baristas showed up. While enjoying wine pilfered from the café, we took turns talking about what we liked and hated about that particular workplace. We concluded that, like the wine, everything we loved about the job came from our own initiatives, not from the bosses. And everything we hated—the recent clampdowns, changes in the scheduling process, overseer-style management—could be navigated with the right solidarity.

We decided to make working there worth it. Most of us already hooked up our friends, but we wanted to connect with other people working in similar situations and formalize the network of service-worker hookups. We also wanted to get paid more; we decided that the workers on each shift would figure out what their needs were, do the math, and make their tips reach that minimum by putting the money from some orders in the tip jar rather than the cash register. We decided that we all deserved to eat; since our shifts interfered with mealtimes, we would also take money from the till to pay for food. In short, we agreed to treat the café as our private domain, and to initiate new co-workers into this secret society.

We transformed the café right under the bosses' noses; for a couple years life was a little more bearable. Eventually, however, someone ran his mouth to the wrong person.

When I got fired—that is, when they quietly dropped my name from the schedule—we had a meeting to figure out what to do. Someone suggested we go on strike; we all laughed despairingly. All of us understood the logic of striking, but our condition was already extremely precarious. We imagined that there was an army of good workers at the gates just aching to be managed by our stupid bosses—workers who thought that stealing was wrong and didn't care about standing up for themselves because they "were only planning on being there for a short while" anyway.

So we lost that round. Eventually the bosses got their finances settled; they even succeeded in producing a few "professional baristas" whose dearest wish was to become a picture in *Barista Magazine*.

If nothing else, though, I'd made some good friendships. One coworker I'd initiated into the game became a very close friend, and together we conspired to keep taking on the service industry. We shared an apartment, went to shows and parties, scrawled graffiti around town, and even attended a few demonstrations.

Our network of friends helped him get a similar position at some gluten-free high-end restaurant in a nearby town. However, he was getting more involved in radical subcultures and he ended up quitting and hitting the road. I had already traveled and all I could think about was continuing the fight through which we'd met—but don't get me wrong, I was happy for him. I knew he would keep fighting, too, though both of us were still at a loss as to what we could do to change things. Thinking about it now, he seems emblematic of a common phenomenon: as soon as people are ready to contest their conditions, they're shifted to another position—either by force, like I was, or by choice, like him.

As fate would have it, after he left, our friends finagled me that same position. What's more, the coworkers he'd just left were on the same page as me.

Back to drawing board. There were five of us. We'd all been working in that industry for years. Most of us were approaching our late twenties and had come to the same conclusions. We began to pilfer what we could and look for weak points.

One of us noticed that there was a small nook near where we juiced fruit, conveniently out of sight of the security cameras; instead of hauling the leftovers to the compost, we started tossing them in there. Two other coworkers discovered that they'd independently begun pissing into a hole in the floor in the employee restroom—we weren't allowed to use the restaurant customer toilets. Perhaps it was a coincidence, but the floor in there actually did collapse. "Pee in the hole!" became the collective anthem for the war we were going to bring to our bosses.

It wouldn't be easy. This business employed a more complex framework of control apparatuses than anywhere any of us had worked before. There were five managers, two on shift at a time. The boss was almost always lurking somewhere—and if he wasn't around, he watching us on the security cameras through his iPhone! The register had to be counted out each shift; if it was off, they took the difference out of your tips. When you learned how to count the money in the drawer, the managers would impose their logic by calling the drawer "you" and talking about how much "you" owed the store.

Even when we weren't at work, they tried to control everything we did. My previous café had done the same thing by sending us to competitions and encouraging us to raise consciousness about espresso, but this was worse. When we talked to the bosses, we had to use expressions like "synergy," "excellent product," "professional atmosphere." Presenting our résumés once wasn't enough—we had to be in character all the time. But the thing that really pushed us over the edge was when they made us use a website to self-manage our own schedules.

This sounds good at first, right? In fact, we already worked out our schedules together, though they usually rejected what we came up with. But shifting scheduling to a website was far more insidious than it sounds.

Imagine what this meant for workers who didn't have their own internet access. Many employees now had to go to the public library on their days off just to find out if they'd been rescheduled to work that night. It wasn't enough that you had to ask for a day off two months in advance—now you also had to petition for it online. And in addition to managing scheduling, the website also stored a cache of digital training videos and store announcements. They paid us the same wage, only without tips, to make these videos for them—giving them permanent tools with which they could produce more baristas and profits in the future. We could lose our jobs, but the videos we'd made would go on earning them money indefinitely.

In addition, now we had no excuse for not knowing all about everything we sold—it was all on the website. Furthermore, the bosses expected us to create avatars and profiles so we could use the website like it was a Facebook for wage slavery.

We talked endlessly about it, venting and trying to work out the best way to respond. If our jobs dominated every part of our lives, why shouldn't our resistance? We made a few more friends at work and began meeting over drinks and whispering to each other during smoke breaks. We were starting to experience a sense of camaraderie, to take ourselves seriously. A couple of us had read about union workers fighting strikebreakers in the 1930s; maybe the formation of the old labor movement had been something like this.

Finally, we made a plan. We would anonymously demand that the bosses abolish the website and discontinue the security cameras or else face a strike by Day X. Knowing that most of our other coworkers would get behind the former demand while the bosses would never go for the latter, we planned a strike that would go beyond the ordinary.

We had already learned a valuable lesson from a coworker who had acted out individually without hope of personal gain. One Saturday night the main cook had just walked out; the boss had to scramble to fill his place and the place lost thousands of dollars. We imagined that if the credit card machine went down it might have a similar effect.

If a strike halts production, sabotage is also a kind of strike. We hypothesized that because what we produced was above all an atmosphere—an environment of care, professionalism, and excellence—we should interrupt those elements of our work. When factory workers who produce material goods go on strike, they refuse to pull levers, move crates, or work the assembly line; we would refuse to fulfill our role of *service*.

We also imagined that our demands could be achieved immediately even if our bosses didn't cave in. The security cameras were all connected through a computer network; that was how the boss could watch them from his iPhone. We contacted some friends who knew a bit about hacking and they offered to block the cameras during the strike.

The strike itself would rely on a minority taking an active role, with most employees simply staying silent about what they saw. Our plan was to continue working but to do everything wrong. Food runners would deliver to the wrong tables. Asked how they were doing, servers would answer customers, "I've been really depressed ever since my friend overdosed." Finally, a few of us would have accidents: a cut hand from slicing fruit here, a fall down the stairs there. Our plan was to make everything stop functioning, including ourselves. We would cost them the entire night and ruin their reputation.

Did we expect to win? It was hard to say. What does it mean to win, anyway? If we'd just wanted better working conditions, we could have gone back to filling out job applications. No, we wanted something else—we wanted to set a new precedent for standing up for ourselves. Even if our strike failed and our demands weren't met, it would be a step towards building an insurgent service sector. By themselves, strikes like ours might not bring about specific changes, but we imagined that they could add up to something much bigger. If we could make a restaurant uncontrollable, what else could we do?

Domestic Labor

"When capital pays husbands they get two workers, not one."
— Selma James

Picture a bourgeois dinner party: the husbands talk about production, the wives about consumption. In this image, men are associated with creating value, women with expending it: *from each according to his ability, to each according to her need.* Every husband has a routine about his spouse using up his hard-earned money—on what, he can't imagine.

But could the economy function without all the unwaged labor of homemakers? Employers have to compensate workers for their labor, but no one compensates homemakers for everything they do to produce and prepare workers. Those saddled with child-rearing, cooking, cleaning, and house-keeping have to depend on the charity of wage-earners—a condition that often traps them in abusive relationships—or else become wage-earners themselves.

So long as women face glass ceilings in the workplace and are expected to do the majority of the labor at home, employment offers no relief. Millions of women have to work for lower wages than men receive for the same jobs, then come home to a second shift of unpaid labor taking care of their homes and families. To this second shift we could add a third shift of emotional care, conflict mediation, and sex, which are often disproportionately *work* for one party.

As sure as capitalists profit on workers' labor, they benefit from this free domestic labor. Imagine if they had to pay to nurse, raise, cook, and clean for every employee! Just as wage slavery proved more sustainable than chattel slavery because it imposes these costs directly onto wage slaves, it's cheapest for employers to leave such tasks to workers' families.

This profitable state of affairs is maintained by a web of political and social institutions dividing labor into waged and unwaged—into *productive* and *reproductive*. The role of housewife is perpetuated by laws and customs that systematically force women out of public life and deny them access to resources. Some of these can be traced back hundreds or thousands of years. Capitalism is not the oldest system that generates imbalances in power, nor the most fundamental; it developed on the foundations laid by patriarchy and other hierarchies. It's impossible to fight these in isolation: a sexist anticapitalism would still create imbalances in access to capital, just as a capitalist feminism would only impose the burdens of exploitation on poorer women.

Speaking of which, many women *do* get paid for child care and domestic work—but not for taking care of their own families. Working-class mothers often have to pay half their income for low-quality child care so they can attend to rich people's kids. Thanks to the women's movement of the 1960s and 1970s, more middle class women can enter the job market and pay other women to clean their houses.

Just like child care, care of the sick and old has largely been absorbed into the market in the form of hospitals, rest homes, and hospices. Thus capitalism distributes care itself, like everything else, according to wealth rather than need.

As it is at work . . .
. . . so it is at home.

The Sex Industry

To prostitute oneself: we can learn a lot about capitalism from this expression. "To put one's talents to an unworthy use for the sake of financial gain": who *doesn't* do that nowadays? But businessmen and professors are not called *prostitutes,* however unworthy the uses they put their talents to; that disgrace is projected onto women and gender renegades too poor to be called "escorts." As with domestic labor, it's frowned upon to demand payment up front for things everyone else sells in a roundabout fashion: it casts too much light on the dynamics at work at every level of society. Sexuality is sacred—that is, the forms it takes and the uses it can be put to are strictly dictated by patriarchal traditions. *Putting one's talents to unworthy use* is attributed to those who are forced to do so to survive, not those who force others to do so.

The ones who profit from the sex industry are not sex workers any more than those who profit from the mining industry are miners. Most of the revenue flows to pornography executives and pimps. Laws that are ostensibly intended to defend public morality and "protect" women chiefly serve to control one of the only industries in which women and others singled out for their sexuality could have an advantage. What does it say about public morality that it is legal to cut the tops off mountains, but illegal for women to resist poverty by taking money for sex?

Meanwhile, "successful" sex workers play the role of showing that the best way to get ahead is to submit to the sexual whims of men. This is just as true of Madonna, Angelina Jolie, and others who sell themselves on sex appeal as it is of outright porn stars. The notion that sex work can be empowering is a version of the myth that capitalism produces democracy and freedom. It's certainly better to get paid $80 an hour rather than $8, but it's still *work*. Most "empowered" sex workers owe their earnings to a patriarchal construction of sexuality that systematically disempowers women, just as worker-owned co-ops still rely on the capitalist market and the exploitation inherent in it for survival.

The sex industry offers an instructive microcosm of the interplay between technological development, social alienation, and capitalist exploitation. Less than a hundred years ago, sex work remained in a pre-industrial phase of development, consisting chiefly of face-to-face encounters between individuals. In the 20th century, new technology enabled capitalists to amass capital in the form of pornographic movies: they could pay sex workers a one-time employment fee in return for a product with which they make a continuous profit. Pornography was already thousands of years old, of course—what was new was the capability to mass-produce realistic simulacra. Just as factories had changed the rest of the economy, this speeded up the process by which sex industry profiteers accumulated capital. It also gave the companies that produced these movies a tremendous influence over the sexuality of millions of consumers—they were not just selling sexual gratification, but also constructing it.

Subsequent technological developments have continued to shape consumer sexuality. In much of the "developed" world, the majority of men's sexual encounters now take place with machines, or at least are mediated by them. Modern sexuality is so focused on the virtual that in real-life liaisons the participants tend to act out roles propagated by the sex industry. In this regard, pornography reifies centuries-old gender roles even as it updates and adjusts them. Over the past few generations the range of recognized sexual practices and gender identities has diversified, but none of these is beyond the influence of capitalism—from an economist's perspective, this is simply a matter of new niche markets opening up.

The imperatives of profit don't just shape the social construction of sex and gender; they also shape their biological construction. Viagra, testosterone, birth control pills: gender is produced in the laboratories of pharmaceutical companies no less than in older institutions like the family. This goes for athletes who take steroids as well as people who get silicon implants. Gender isn't just used to push product lines—it is simultaneously a consumer identity, a commodity, and an aspect of the project of *selling oneself* that goes on even outside the workplace.

In this context, deviation from constructed gender norms has been appropriated as a medical phenomenon to confirm that those norms are more "natural" than the bodies into which we're born. By promoting a narrative in which transsexuals are women trapped in men's bodies and vice versa, psychiatric and medical authorities imply that the categories *man* and *woman* are universal and exhaustive. Paradoxically, in enabling people to pass between supposedly immutable categories, they cement the hegemony of the patriarchal two-gender system—and the exclusion of anyone who can't or won't choose a side.

Thus, from pleasure to gender identity, capitalism influences the most intimate details of every aspect of life. Facets of ourselves that once developed outside its dictates are colonized by the market until we can only access them through it: for example, the man who finds it difficult to masturbate without mainstream pornography. When sexuality is fashioned by economic forces and sexual relations often occur between partners with differing access to resources, it can be hard to distinguish sex work from sex, period.

Military, Police, and Private Security

"I can hire one half of the working class to kill the other half."
– Financier Jay Gould

As Chicago mayor Richard Daley explained about the riots at the 1968 Democratic National Convention, "the policeman isn't there to create disorder—the policeman is there to *preserve* disorder."

The more unequal the distribution of resources and power, the more force it takes to maintain it. We can see this in macrocosm in the military occupation of entire nations and in microcosm in the security guard in the grocery store, following up one tour of duty with another. Every day the National Security Agency intercepts and stores almost two billion emails and phone calls; surveillance cameras point at the cash register in every gas station. This speaks volumes about how balanced our society is.

One might ask what good all this apparatus is when domestic violence and poor-on-poor crime continue unabated. But the point is not to prevent violence so much as to monopolize control: so long as it doesn't pose a threat to the balance of power, violence isn't a priority for the police. Chaos and violence often increase in response to repressive force, but this can legitimize the occupiers and divide the occupied.

The contradictions inherent in capitalism help to sustain it. Capitalism produces poor people who lack jobs; they are offered jobs policing other poor people, at home or abroad. The military is by far the most socialized sector of the US economy. Without the employment opportunities it offers the poor and restless, many of them might seek their fortune in *another army.*

The armed forces don't just enforce imbalances—they also impose new ones. Military interventions like the Opium Wars and the invasion of Iraq deliver labor and resources to the victors cheap. Occupations, political coups, proxy wars, and subtler pressures to "democratize" are all means of securing territory for business. This is why the majority of the budget of the US government goes to the military: the state functions as a collective pooling of resources to implement capitalist interests, and the military is among the most important tools in this toolbox.

In theory, of course, soldiers and police exist to protect citizens from other armed thugs. In that regard, they run a sort of protection racket, as citizens may legitimately have even more to fear from other thugs than they do from the ones who serve their rulers. This situation serves the rulers just fine: the more their subjects fear other nations—or each other—the less they'll object to their own subjugation.

Open warfare was relatively common in the days when governments conceived of their interests as distinct nations rather than participants in a global economy. Nowadays, international conflicts are often framed as a global majority attempting to rein in a "rogue state" such as Iraq or North Korea. Rather than fighting for ascendancy, governments increasingly work together to deepen and fortify the foundations of capitalism. Consequently, old-fashioned wars have been replaced by *policing* on a global scale, while policing has escalated into *war on the population*: wars on drugs, on "terrorism," on illegal immigration, on political dissent.

In fact, although armies have been around for millennia, police are relatively new. Until recently, communities generally regulated themselves. The wealthy and powerful sometimes brought in mercenaries to "keep the peace," but they were chiefly concerned with protecting their own privileges and punishing insubordination. Their intrusions into poor communities were infrequent and obvious.

When modern police departments appeared in the 18th and 19th centuries, it was not to make communities safer but to subordinate them to a central authority. This was one of many initiatives to extend bureaucratic control into every aspect of life. Previously, the disobedient had been able to take advantage of conflicts between rival factions of the power structure. Now resisting the police meant pitting yourself against the entire apparatus of the state.

The industrial revolution concentrated the exploited and the goods they produced in chaotic urban environments in which many of them attempted to enact a freelance redistribution of wealth. In this situation, capitalists could no longer protect their interests on a piecemeal basis. So the introduction of centralized police served two purposes: it monopolized state control, while protecting property and trade for merchants and industrialists—which in turn produced tax revenues for the state. Accordingly, police focused on preventing theft and "idleness," though then as now they used sensationalized stories of violent crime to justify their existence.

Many of the techniques these police utilized had originally been developed by royal spies to suppress seditious ideas and conspiracies. This was no coincidence: as the fortunes of the state came to depend on capitalist accumulation, popular crimes against private property became one of the greatest threats to the power structure.

So at bottom, political repression and crime prevention serve the same purpose. Shrewd police spokesmen can shift their rhetoric seamlessly from fighting crime to fighting political extremism and back again according to what is most convenient. When political movements buy into these categories and do the work of distinguishing themselves from "criminals," they save police the trouble of intervening.

Today, as more and more "public" space is privately owned—malls, campuses, gated communities—private companies and other nongovernmental groups are increasingly responsible for the day-to-day tasks of crime prevention. There are now over one million security guards in the US; they outnumber police officers. Meanwhile, businesses often contract specific services from police for a fee, or provide police facilities in exchange for increased patrols. In some areas, non-profit organizations and police recruit civilians to monitor their own neighborhoods.

Rather than a return to the days before police, this represents a new stage in the expansion of policing. Centralized police forces became necessary during a time of upheaval when the majority of people didn't identify with capitalism; they served to create a homogeneous environment in which commerce could flourish. They still function to suppress upheavals—hence the shift towards SWAT teams and crowd control tactics. But now that capitalism has subjugated most of the world, privatized and decentralized policing has an

advantage: it can adapt to specific contexts without being limited by overarching frameworks like law or justice. Like work itself, policing has become flexible and diversified.

Similarly, as the nation-state ceases to be the principle actor in international politics, state militaries are once again being supplemented with private mercenaries. Commercial security agencies are contracted overseas while state militaries are brought home to put down revolts in their own nations.

In an era of increasing unemployment, police are to the excluded what bosses are to workers. As the front line imposing the inequalities of property rights they are often the primary target for the rage of the dispossessed. Whenever this rage boils over enough to threaten those inequalities, we see that every state is a police state in waiting.

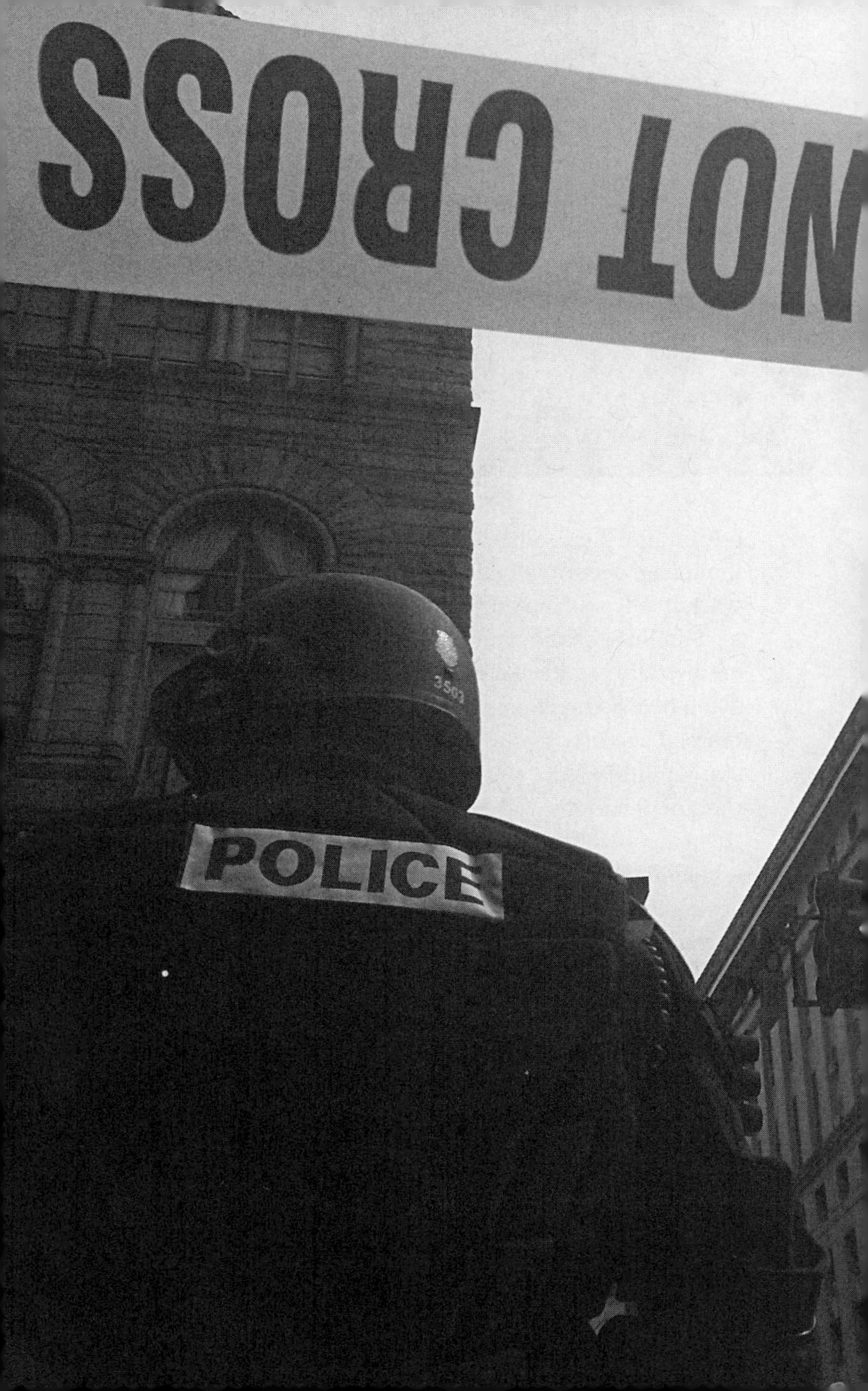
NOT CROSS
POLICE

CRIME SCENE DO

Must we stress once again that we're here to safeguard your freedom?

Migrant Labor

Why do people cross borders illegally looking for work? Doesn't this show that the US and the European Union have better economies than places like Mexico and Morocco? Don't they have a right to defend them against interlopers?

This is nonsense—it's all the *same* economy. Commodities, jobs, and profits flow effortlessly across borders that are enforced chiefly upon human beings, the better to exploit them. Not only the borders but the nations themselves are arbitrary constructs, just like the designation "illegal immigrant"—together, these serve to legitimize the segregation of the workforce into castes. But to get to the bottom of all this, we have to start a few centuries back.

When the conquistadors first set sail, their top priority was to obtain resources with which to gain the upper hand in the power struggles back home. Wherever they found hierarchical societies, they deposed the local ruling class and put themselves in its place; wherever the locals were more difficult to rule, they displaced or butchered them. The parts of the world that were richest in biodiversity—the tropics and rainforests—were treated as treasure troves to be looted; to this day those regions of the earth remain the poorest and most exploited. Cooler regions with less to plunder, such as North America, ended up receiving Europe's excess population. Eventually these became wealthy nations themselves, because wealth stayed there rather than being sent back

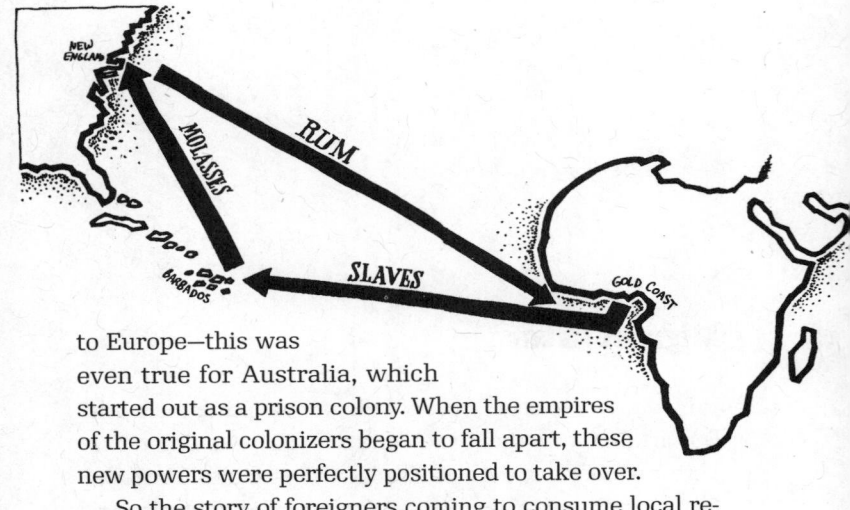

to Europe—this was
even true for Australia, which
started out as a prison colony. When the empires
of the original colonizers began to fall apart, these
new powers were perfectly positioned to take over.

So the story of foreigners coming to consume local resources and funnel money out of the economy is a projection: it is exactly what colonizers have done to migrant laborers' homelands for centuries. Every time a US corporation sets up an outlet in a foreign country and sends the profits home, the same process of exploitation that occurs between an employer and a wage laborer recurs between nations. The International Monetary Fund and World Bank can force "structural adjustment programs" on so-called developing nations in return for loans precisely because these countries have been exploited for so long.

Migrant labor is an inevitable result of this uneven "development," and it's hardly a new phenomenon. In the United States, for example, Chinese immigrants were brought in after the abolition of slavery to maintain the cotton industry and construct the transcontinental railroads. Racist laws denied them citizenship and land-owning rights and eventually forced tens of thousands of them out of the country, but they were soon replaced by Mexican laborers.

The following century saw alternating waves of immigration and expulsion of Mexicans, who were brought in for cheap labor during both world wars and then expelled during the subsequent economic downturns. Border control was originally a responsibility of the Department of Labor, a means of controlling labor surpluses. Even where government regulations were supposed to protect migrant laborers, employers would sidestep the laws to cut costs and migrant laborers would go along out of economic necessity.

In the 1980s, the collapse of the Mexican economy forced small landowners to sell their property and seek employment; maquiladoras appeared in the northern part of the country to take advantage of this cheap labor and avoid US environmental and labor regulations. A decade later, the same factors drew some of these factories to East Asia, forcing laborers to continue north to the farms and meat-packing plants of the US. Today East Asians also work as migrant laborers, some in more recently wealthy regions such as the Arabian peninsula.

Letting laborers into a nation only long enough to work—forbidding them to stay afterwards or bring their families with them—is a way to extract maximum labor at minimum cost. Even if the laborers take all their earnings home after living expenses, the employers still profit more on their labor than they could on local workers, and the government doesn't have to pay for schools or social services for their children or parents. The same goes for day labor, in which employers only pay for the hours of work they need without covering employee benefits or dead time on the clock. Undocumented immigrants who have to work under the table are already fulfilling the "libertarian" capitalist dream of an unregulated market. So it is that those whose homelands were pillaged by colonizers must deliver themselves to the colonizers' doorsteps again for further pillaging.

Non-citizens, "illegal" or not, make especially vulnerable employees even when they don't come from plundered nations. They lack the protections granted to citizens; if they try to organize, they can be fired outright, even deported.

Consequently, they have often been used to break up strikes and unions, which has also served to foster racist divisions in the workforce.

Penalties for employers who hire illegal immigrants just drive down wages for migrant laborers—from the employers' perspective, the risk is only worth it if it cuts costs, while the laborers need the jobs at practically any wage. Likewise, border enforcement doesn't keep undocumented immigrants out so much as trap them in: if they need the work, they'll find a way to cross the border for it, but without hope of easily returning home. This creates a permanently marginalized population inside the US that no longer has to be enticed across the border by specific job offers. Today there are something like 12 million illegal immigrants in the US, many of whom have been here for much of their lives.

The converse of migrant labor is outsourcing, in which the labor itself migrates but the workers stay where they are. Thanks to new technologies, corporations don't have to go to the "developing world" to plunder it, nor entice its laborers here—they can employ them at cut-rate prices wherever they are.

Today, as peoples of different nations are increasingly intermixed, the world economy is divided into *zones of privilege* that are not enforced along spatial lines so much as along lines of identity. Some of these are coded into law and enforced by documentation; others are imposed chiefly by economic or social structures. In this context, nationality supplements the class system with an old-fashioned caste system, legally restricting the rights and movements of poor Mexican workers unless they marry into a higher caste. This is one of the many ways the workforce has been fragmented in order to maximize its vulnerability to exploitation.

Conquer, pillage, and employ the survivors at bargain prices

AFTER ABOUT TWO HOURS we stopped in a side canyon to dress some of the girl's wounds. "How old are you?" I asked her.

"Fifteen. I've lived in Oregon since I was two. What am I going to do in Mexico? I've never lived there. I don't have any people there. I haven't been able to get hold of my parents since I got deported. I'm just going to have to keep trying this until I make it."

They had been utterly lost for four days and nights. The Salvadoran had a cell phone, which got no service in the US. It was full of pictures of places they had been and things they had seen. "Look at this mountain," he urged. "We crossed it! It was so beautiful. We thought for sure that we were going to die."

While they were recuperating he asked me how much it cost to fill up the tank of my truck. I told him usually about seventy-five bucks.

"Seventy-five? Dollars?"

"Yeah," I affirmed, assuming he thought that this was very expensive. "How much would it cost in El Salvador?"

"A hundred and fifty, maybe two hundred."

"Two hundred? Dollars? Jesus! How much do you make an hour there?"

"I was making eight dollars a day working construction when I left."

I got a pencil and we did some math. After lengthy calculations we determined three things:

1) A hundred and fifty to two hundred dollars a tank represents about twenty days of labor at eight dollars a day.

2) I usually make about fifteen dollars an hour, which is about a hundred and twenty dollars a day.

3) This meant that a one-hundred-and-seventy-five-dollar tank of gas for the Salvadoran was as difficult to pay for as a twenty-five-hundred-dollar tank of gas would be for me.

"That's a problem," I said.

"It's a very serious problem," he agreed. "They tied our currency to the dollar, and everything got incredibly expensive. It's just impossible to live there right now."

He called me a week later from his cousin's house in Utah. They had made it out of the desert.

Prisoners

What is the function of prisons? Above all, to keep people docile *in other prisons*. Prisons are necessary not to preserve order so much as to protect and enforce the inequalities produced by the market. The coercion and control they represent isn't an aberration in an otherwise free society, but the essential precondition for capitalism. Prisons are simply a more extreme manifestation of the same logic inherent in property rights and national borders.

The US currently has the world's highest incarceration rate, with over 2.4 million people in prisons and detention facilities and 5 million more on probation or parole. The majority are serving time for property crimes or participation in illegal capitalist enterprises. The prison industry itself is increasingly integral to the US economy: it offers inmate labor for less than a dollar an hour, provides opportunities to sell products to inmates and governments alike, and employs hundreds of thousands of prison guards who would otherwise face bleak career prospects.

Nearly half of all prisoners are black, though black people comprise a much smaller percentage of the total US population; one can trace the lineage of the prison system directly to the institution of slavery. In some cases this link is obvious: the Louisiana State Penitentiary still functions as a cotton plantation the way it did before the Civil War, when the fields were worked by slaves rather than prisoners serving life sentences.

It's easy to see all this as racist profiteering, pure and simple, but there's more to it. Prisons are fundamentally a way to deal with the structural challenges inherent in capitalism.

As capitalists accumulate more and more wealth, the exploited and excluded have less and less reason to obey property laws. Before the establishment of the modern prison system, much of the urban population participated in "criminal" practices, or sympathized with those who did; to solve this problem, it was necessary to isolate disobedience in a *criminal element* that could be quarantined and controlled. The prison system and all the attending forms of punishment and surveillance combine to institutionalize a division between worker and delinquent, embodying this in cultural and ethical frameworks as well as the physical segregation of bodies. Like other divisions—wage laborer and slave, citizen and immigrant—this division is calculated to fracture the interests of those on the wrong side of capitalism. To the "honest" worker, the problems of criminals are their own affair—and their own fault.

So prisons are one aspect of the project of creating a criminal class, which is essential to industrial capitalism. It's no coincidence that the modern prison system appeared at the time of the industrial revolution. This also explains why recidivism is always a "problem" but never solved: the more distinct the criminal class, the easier it is to control. Once this criminal class is divided from the rest of the population and set at odds with it, all crime is experienced as antisocial, and workers consider their enemies to be the criminals who might steal from them rather than the capitalists who do so constantly.

Prisons also serve to manage the exploited and excluded in other ways. Transitions from one mode of production to another often require a tremendous influx of cheap labor and resources: for example, Britain was only able to industrialize as a result of plundering its overseas colonies. At the same

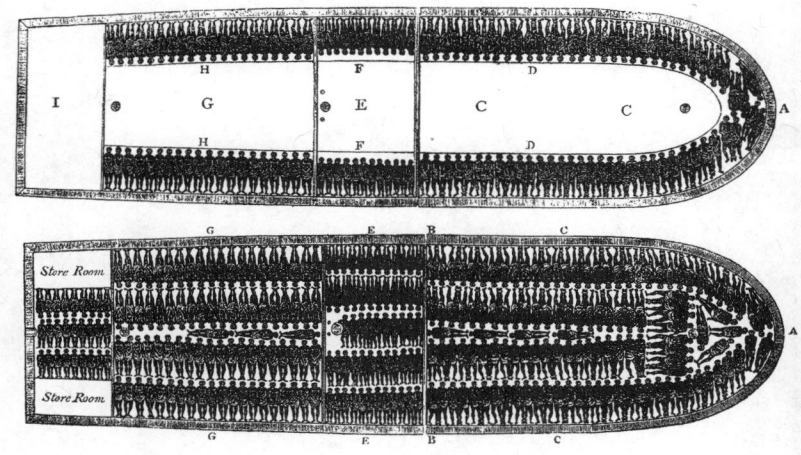

Prisons: *slave ships on dry land*

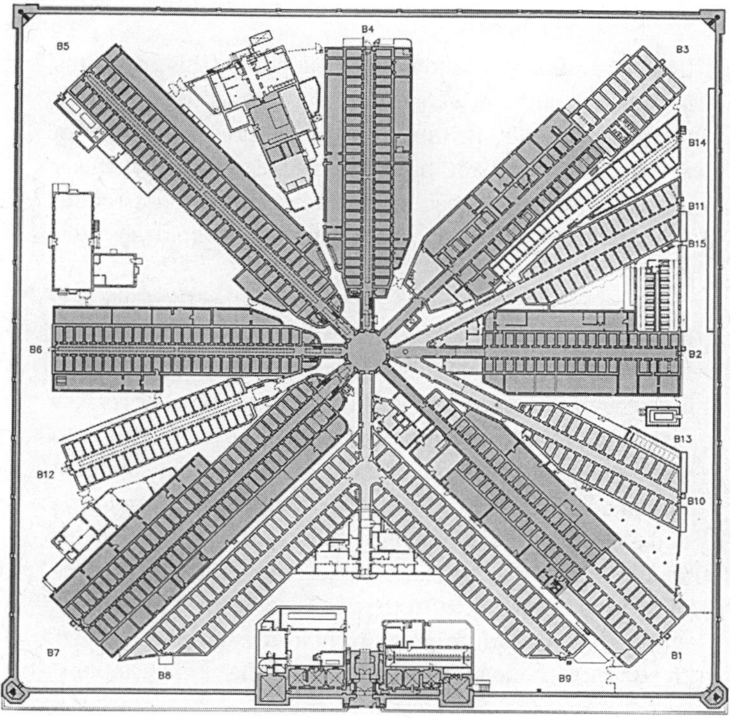

time, as production becomes more efficient, this generates a surplus population whose labor is no longer needed—such as the "criminals" Britain exported to prison colonies in Australia. The prison industry can solve either of these problems, forcibly conscripting cheap labor or controlling those who have been excluded from the economy. It often does both at once.

Thus, convict leasing was instituted after the Civil War as a way to obtain free labor, control the population of newly freed slaves, and speed the industrialization of the South. Two generations later, the Bolsheviks seized power overseas on the platform that state control was the swiftest way to industrialize Russia and catch up with Western capitalist nations. This industrialization demanded the plundering and eventual imprisonment of millions: first as a means of accumulating wealth for the state, then in order to force or intimidate people into new economic roles. The Nazis employed a similar program in their attempts to revitalize the German economy, as did a series of "developing nations" on both sides of the Iron Curtain after the Second World War. In this way many former colonies of industrialized Western nations managed to kick-start their transition to a new mode of production by treating their own citizens the same way foreign imperialists had.

In the long run, it turned out that robbing and imprisoning people was more effective for initiating economic growth than for maintaining it. The Soviet Union and other state-capitalist countries eventually shifted to the free market model, which offered more incentives for competition while maintaining the hierarchies that developed during so-called socialism.

But prisons are as essential to free-market capitalism as they are to state capitalism. As the industrialization of poorer nations enticed companies to move their factories in pursuit of cheap labor and technological innovations replaced other jobs entirely, a new class appeared in the US that was extraneous to production. This coincided with the forceful suppression of the black and brown liberation movements of the 1960s. What could be done to keep this newly redundant and volatile class under control? The answer was a skyrocketing prison population.

Today there are as many people behind bars in the United States as there were in the Soviet gulags at the height of Stalin's power. That's more than the entire US military, including reserves. The prison industry imposes unprecedented levels of surveillance and control, but it creates a social body that has nothing to gain from the continuation of capitalism.

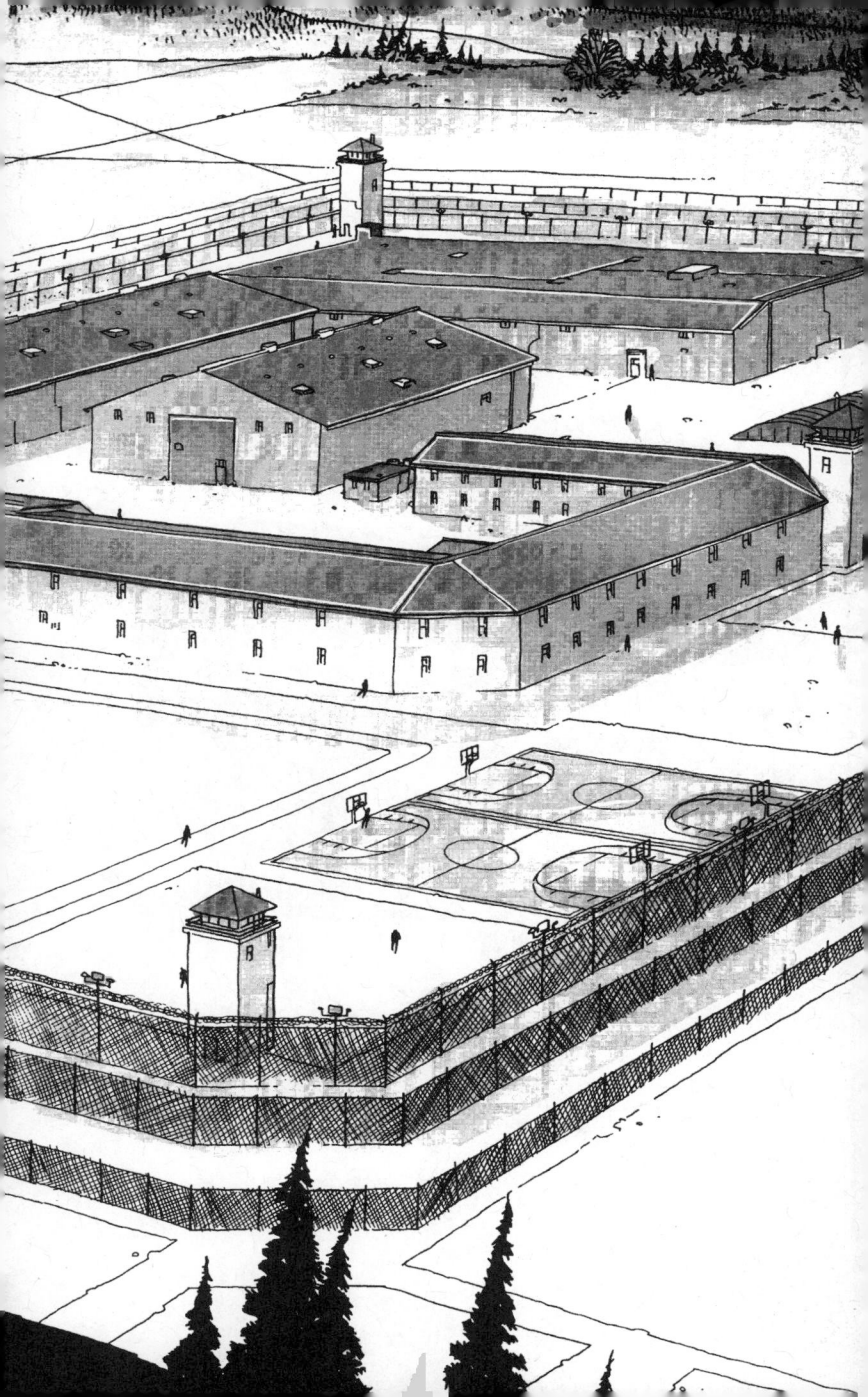

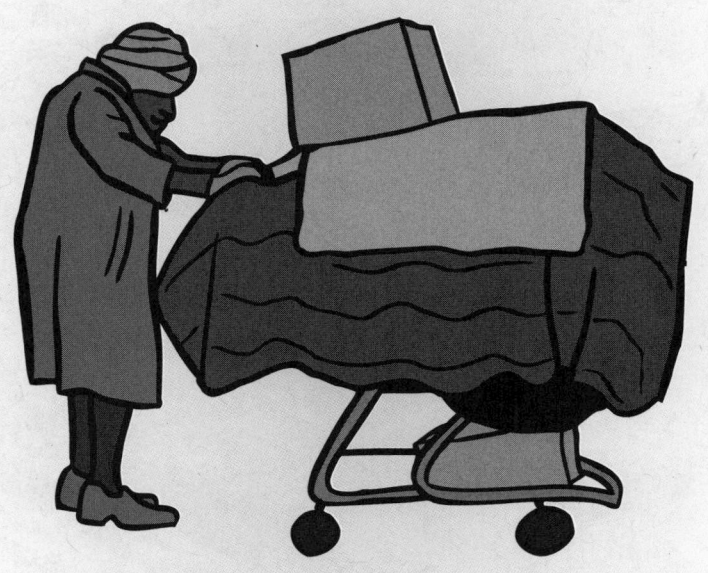

Unemployment and Homelessness

Is there anything worse than prison? There must be—some people try to get into prison to survive the winter.

On the market, human beings can depreciate like any commodity. The laws of supply and demand apply to labor too: the more workers available, the cheaper employers can get them. An unemployed population serves the dual purpose of keeping wages down and reminding employees to be careful not to wind up on the wrong side of a pink slip. The unemployed suffer the double humiliation of having to beg for humiliating jobs; this confuses everything by making them seem eager to be exploited, when in fact it's simply the lesser of two evils.

A century ago, champions of technological progress proclaimed that it would liberate human beings from the need to work, creating a new leisure society. But although these new technologies have indeed eliminated jobs, this has largely been used to save employers money, not to provide for the general public. From the perspective of the unemployed, free time and access to resources seem to be concentrated at opposite poles of the economic spectrum. Some leisure society!

Capitalism produces wealth, but it produces *far more* poverty. There's no upper limit to how much wealth one individual can amass, but there is a lower limit to how much any one person can be pillaged—so it takes a tremendous number of poor people to produce a few billionaires.

Unemployment is one form of exclusion from the market; homelessness is another, and all the different forms reinforce each other in a feedback loop. In the US, well over a million people are homeless; worldwide, over a billion live in favelas, refugee camps, and worse. We think of shantytowns as the periphery of cities, but in some countries the majority of the population dwells in them. Most of the new arrivals to these shantytowns are not driven by the availability of work but by the destruction of their traditional ways of life. With the need for labor in manufacturing steadily declining, slums function as a holding pool for the unwanted in regions where there's not enough wealth to support a large service sector. The point is to keep them within reach of sweatshops and processing plants but out of range of the wealthy.

Like the unemployed, the excluded play a role in capitalism simply by implying the consequences of exclusion. But this is not enough—for economic success to be associated with personal merit, it has to appear that exclusion is *their fault*. Divested of all assets and hope, the poor can be made to look vicious enough. Yet not so long ago, before private ownership, access to resources was evenly distributed among all human beings; if some people and peoples are impoverished now, it is because they—or their ancestors—were *looted*. One need only open a history book to read about the brutal history of colonialism in the Americas, Africa, India, China—but this process continues today wherever one person's labor enriches another.

Some people chafe at welfare programs funded by tax dollars: why should someone else get a free ride off their hard work? They ought to ask the same question about politicians and bosses. In fact, every poor person who has ever worked for a wage has helped give the wealthy a free ride. Tax money that goes to welfare is one of the only examples of wealth flowing back down the pyramid to the class that does most of the work to create it. Welfare programs were

"There is one kind of prison where the man is behind bars, and everything that he desires is outside; and there is another kind where the things are behind the bars, and the man is outside."
- Upton Sinclair

won by decades of bitter struggle; wherever the powerful do not fear an impending uprising of the poor, they are dismantling them.

That's not to say that public assistance programs could ever be an effective solution to the ills of capitalism. Welfare programs and charity organizations both tend to foster middle-class bureaucracies while shaming and disempowering the needy. Welfare and charity only redistribute wealth on the terms of the wealthy—that is, as a means of maintaining the unequal balance of power. Welfare programs in particular are interconnected with the same apparatus of control used to repress poor people who get out of line: they use the same databases, impose the same compulsory programs, and treat the poor with the same lack of respect. The only real cure for poverty is for the poor to seize resources back on their own terms.

The tactics available to the excluded tend towards revolt rather than reform. They can't go on strike, but they can

block traffic like Argentina's *piqueteros*. They can't stage boycotts, but they can walk out of stores en masse without paying. They can't organize rent strikes, but they can occupy buildings and land. As poverty spreads, these tactics will too.

> "Anyone who has worked in, or witnessed, any of the 'anti-poverty' programs in the American ghetto has an instant understanding of 'foreign aid' in the 'underdeveloped' nations. In both locales, the most skillful adventurers improve their material lot; the most dedicated of the natives are driven mad or inactive—or underground—by frustration; while the misery of the hapless, voiceless millions is increased—and not only that: their reaction to their misery is described to the world as criminal."
> – James Baldwin

Outside the Market

On the periphery, some still survive more or less according to pre-capitalist ways of life. Some of these are indigenous peoples fighting to retain their traditions; others are populations of the excluded that have already been absorbed into the economy, chewed up, and spat out. As the market gobbles up more and more, those who subsist outside it have increasingly little to live on. From this vantage point, no one can imagine what life was like when everyone had everything around him at his disposal.

Until recently, much of the human race still derived sustenance directly from the land immediately beneath their feet. This provided a safety net in hard times. Now almost everyone has to go through the market to get the things they need to survive—making economic recessions as dangerous as earthquakes and tsunamis, even though they're entirely artificial. And while natural disasters pass, capitalism persists: famines are temporary, but poverty is enduring.

Yet even today some part of every person's life remains outside the logic of profit and competition: relationships with friends and family, for example, or the breeze on a summer day. The best things in life are still free. Activities that are fulfilling in and of themselves, sharing without keeping score—these are still essential to our society, whether they take the form of neighborhood sports or open-source software. A lot of this is quarantined to narrow social contexts, occurring only between equals the same way the ancient Athenians practiced democracy among themselves while keeping slaves. But it's telling that even the wealthiest people, the ones most anxious to protect their privileges, still prefer to relate to others this way when they can. It's hard to imagine *everything* being swallowed by the economy, however colonized we become.

On the other hand, those who try to flee the market rarely make it far. The most remote communes still have to own or rent space, pay taxes, and deal with the ways the participants retain capitalist values and emotional damage. In the long run, this kind of autonomy can foster the same sort of values as self-employment. Attempted on the margins of capitalist society, under incredible pressure and influence from it, autonomous spaces tend to present an impoverished model of what another world might be. At worst, they serve to demoralize participants—sending the message that their utopian alternative is doomed to fail and giving the impression that this is their own fault rather than a consequence of capitalist power. The spaces that survive often turn inward, losing hope of catalyzing broader change.

Such escape attempts have sometimes served to spread capitalism further, as in the case of the European refugees who fled to the so-called New World. Yet in those days, deserters could still cross the frontier and join non-capitalist communities—and they often did, fighting alongside them against their former kinsmen. Today, the frontiers have been pushed to the very edges of the earth. Those who wish to escape capitalism have to fight where they stand.

Animals, Plants, Minerals

Animals—and also plants, minerals, and *everything else*—are treated the same way we are by the economy. Holding a hamburger in his hand, the worker looks into a mirror and beholds the tremendous potential of another being's life forcibly reduced to a commodity. That goes for the vegan alternative: soybean monoculture inflicts the same damage and homogenization as factory farming. The corpses of billions of living things are heaped at the base of the pyramid of the economy. Visiting a slaughterhouse or vivisection lab, it's easy to imagine the living species envying the extinct ones.

Neither glaciers nor the mountaintops they rest on are safe from the demands of the market. The earth itself is being systematically transformed into the waste products of profit. This is the ultimate result of the institution of private property and the motives it produces: living creatures are reduced to objects and the material world is subordinated to self-fulfilling superstitions.

Non-humans are still shoveled into the economy without the benefit of a contract the way non-Europeans were until recently. A few are permitted to retain a little autonomy for the amusement of consumers: national forests, wildlife for hunting and fishing, domesticated animals. The same zones of privilege that divide human society separate other species too: Leona Helmsley's dog inherits millions of dollars while cows and pigs are slaughtered by the billion.

Looking at our fellow creatures as mere playing pieces for power struggles, it's easy to forget that not so long ago human beings experienced themselves as a part of the natural world. That world still offers hints of what life is like without economics. Walking in an old-growth forest, you can begin to imagine how much abundance and diversity we've lost.

"The managers tell us that the swimmers, crawlers, walkers, and fliers spent their lives working in order to eat. These managers are broadcasting their news too soon. The varied beings haven't all been exterminated yet. You, reader, have only to mingle with them, or just watch them from a distance, to see that their waking lives are filled with dances, games, and feasts. Even the hunt, the stalking and feinting and leaping, is not what we call Work, but what we call Fun. The only beings who work are inmates like us."

– Fredy Perlman

Production

Work produces many things—material goods, information, organization, cultural practices, meaning itself. Above all, work produces workers and capitalists, generation after generation. The function of production is not simply to create commodities, but to reproduce the social structures and power relations that give rise to the need to work. In a word, work *produces value* in order to *reproduce values*.

Capitalism is indisputably productive; the incentives and threats of the free market compel ever greater innovation and output. But this can be deceptive. Production doesn't make goods appear out of nowhere; it transforms time, energy, and raw materials into commodities. This is true even of intangible goods such as new computer programs. Although the goods thus produced have a market value, the time and energy and raw materials might have been more valuable by other criteria in their original forms: trees are more valuable to an ecosystem before they are transformed into junk mail, just as a computer programmer might prefer to spend the afternoon with her daughter in the woods. *Production* is one way to describe the process by which everything is being incorporated into the economy: the privatizing of the whole world, tree by tree, labor hour by labor hour, idea by idea, genome by genome.

This is not to say capitalist production never creates goods that would be desirable outside its logic. Our society produces a tremendous surplus beyond what we need to survive; much of this takes the form of useful tools, enjoyable luxuries, expanding knowledge of the cosmos. But these goods also function as status symbols establishing hierarchies and stratifying power—this explains designer clothing and summer houses that sit empty most of the year. They serve to make socially produced inequalities concrete.

Ever-increasing production can obscure the resulting disparities in power. In 1911, only the very wealthy had automobiles; by 2011, there was roughly one passenger car per eleven people worldwide. If you measure quality of life strictly in terms of access to material goods, most people should be better off now. Yet having to sit in traffic to and from work and the grocery store every day is not exactly an improvement for the vast majority; witness the return of the middle class to dense urban areas where cars are less essential. The class that had automobiles in 1911 now has private jets, and all of those vehicles are poisoning the atmosphere at an unprecedented pace—while the people who suffer most from the consequences of all this *still* can't afford cars.

If the essential fabric of human life is not *control over the material world* but *socially produced meanings and relationships,* all this extra production is beside the point. As long as wealth and power are distributed unequally, increased production can only offer limited advantages for the majority; as they come to have proportionately less say in society, things may actually get worse for them.

Production is extending deeper and deeper into the lives of workers. When we imagine what production was like in the 19th century, we picture a worker carrying out orders with his body. Today's worker often has to focus on his duties mind, body, and soul, until he becomes indistinguishable from

I-95 SOUTH
Richmond

EXIT 169 A
Fran...
Fran...
95

EXIT 169 B

EXITS 169B – A

644

Workplace
Junction

1/2 MILE

SEAFOOD

DEER PARK

them. He may not produce physical goods at all, but attention, data, fashion, trends; if he is an entertainer or simply a hip urbanite he may have to sell his own image—never ceasing to be *on the clock.*

The line between production and consumption is blurring as new sectors of the economy absorb the worker's entire being into the task of producing value. For example, in updating her online profile, a student adds content to the internet in a way that produces wealth for a company selling online advertisements.

Much of this cultural and information production goes unpaid, though it still helps channel profit to capitalists. Once, journalists could get paying jobs at small-town newspapers; now those newspapers are being run out of business by bloggers who work for free. Likewise, underground bands used to be able to release their own records and sell them at a modest profit; now if they want anyone to come see them perform, they have to pay out of pocket to record songs to put up on the internet free of charge, essentially submitting a demo directly to the public rather than to corporate record labels. All this free content adds value to the internet itself, filling the pockets of technology magnates like Bill Gates and Steve Jobs who sell the means of accessing it. So long as capitalists control the means of producing material goods, free distribution of information can actually exacerbate social divisions in their favor, eroding the middle class in the information and entertainment industries.

"Free" forms of production are also being explored, such as crowdsourcing, in which volunteers from the general public solve problems and improve products. Both free distribution and volunteer production are perfect for an era of high unemployment, in which it is necessary both to placate the jobless and to make use of them. It's possible that in the future, free volunteer labor will increasingly function as a part of capitalism rather than an opposition to it, as a wealthy elite draws on a vast body of temporary and unemployed workers to maintain its power and their dependence. Most insidious of all, this free labor will appear to benefit the general public rather than the elite.

Ironically, free production and distribution would seem to be the hallmark of any anticapitalist practice. But for these to be able to bring about new power relations, we have to do away with private ownership of capital.

An appendage of flesh on a machine of iron

Consumption

> *"The only thing 'free' about so-called free time is that it doesn't cost the boss anything. Free time is mostly devoted to getting ready for work, going to work, returning from work, and recovering from work. Free time is a euphemism for the peculiar way labor, as a factor of production, not only transports itself at its own expense to and from the workplace, but assumes primary responsibility for its own maintenance and repair. Coal and steel don't do that. Lathes and typewriters don't do that."*
> – Bob Black

For capitalism to function, workers must only be able to access the products of their labor through the market. If they could directly make and take everything they needed, there would be no way for capitalists to profit. This separation between production and consumption is imposed in every transition to capitalism. As capitalism expands and deepens, it becomes a separation between the worker and every aspect of the world she lives in.

Of course, the products of *paid* labor are not the only things that are consumed. European colonizers accused indigenous peoples of cannibalism, sometimes explicitly to justify enslaving them. Yet today, many of those peoples are only remembered in the names of cities and sports teams, while their staple crops and religious traditions are sold in gas stations. Who devoured whom?

Once everyone has been pressed into the market, new dynamics emerge. As production increases, survival itself is subject to a kind of inflation: it takes more and more resources to participate in social life. A few centuries ago, peasant farmers only relied on the exchange economy for a few specific goods; they could grow everything else they needed at home or barter with their neighbors for it. Today's consumer must have a cell phone, a television, a computer, a car, a bank account and credit, insurance, and a great deal more to take part in society, let alone wield any influence in it. If a peasant farmer had miraculously come to possess any of these he would have been rich, but today's consumer can have them all and still be poor. This inflation produces a class of people who are excluded from society in the midst of a great abundance of goods.

The same dynamic plays out on the level of nations and peoples. When one society is scrambling to out-produce and out-invent their neighbors in order to conquer or at least profit off them, everyone else has to rush to keep up; who wants to end up poor and exploited? This pressure was behind much of the destructive industrialization of "developing" nations.

Having become merchandise themselves, workers consume merchandise to exert power the only way they can. Once there is nothing to compare it against, purchasing ceases to be a necessary evil and becomes a sacred act; in the religion of capitalism, in which financial power is equated with social value and spending is thus proof of worth, it is a form of communion. The store is the temple in which the act of buying affirms the consumer's place in society. Much of our leisure time is made up of rituals in which spending money itself is the point: it is what qualifies an activity as *having a good time* or *going on a date*.

In the 20th century, mass production created an increasingly homogeneous consumer culture. But when market expansion reached its limits, capitalists shifted to diversifying consumer options; consequently, the rebellious subcultures that had arisen in reaction to mass society were transformed into market niches. Promoting individuality and "difference" became a formula by which to extend consumerism further and further, capitalizing on the very discontent it produced.

Today there's a product line for every identity—for every ethnic group, sexual preference, and political position. These products have become indistinguishable from the identities they supplement: when the pop star sings about what he likes in a woman, he sings about her perfume, her makeup, her clothes. Even the most rebellious subcultural identities are founded on shared consumption patterns—on shared *aesthetics*.

In a time when economic pressures are constantly breaking up and reconfiguring workforces and local communities, it isn't surprising that people base their sense of self more in their consumer activity than their roles in production. Unruly neighborhoods are gentrified out of existence and rebellious ethnic groups are divided between prison and assimilation; any social body that assumes a radical conception of its interests is dispersed as swiftly as possible. Perhaps this explains why opposition to capitalism is spreading as an ideological identity but diminishing as a force in struggles over production and physical territory. Resistance isn't impossible under these conditions, but it has to assume new forms. Most of the recent innovations in resistance tactics have taken place on the terrain of consumption rather than production: squatting movements, food distribution networks, anticapitalist subcultures.

Meanwhile, every form of resistance that doesn't address the root of the problem is reabsorbed into the functioning of the market. Outrage against specific symptoms of capitalism has generated ethical consumerism, which only serves to stimulate the capitalist economy. For products like free-range chicken and fair-trade coffee, being "ethical" is an additional selling point to increase their perceived value and thus their price. In the free market, selling price is not determined by the material costs of producing the item, but by the highest price consumers will pay. Value is not an inherent characteristic—even petroleum is only valuable inside of a certain social framework. The social construction of "sustainable" and "natural" as desirable characteristics serves to create a new *immaterial value* that can sell items at higher prices even during an economic downturn—utilizing consumers' good intentions to perpetuate the system that gave rise to the problems in the first place. So long as capitalism remains the law of the land, any actual benefit to chickens or Brazilian coffee harvesters can only last as long as it is *profitable*.

this used to be a forest
and everything was free

Media

Taken as a whole, the media functions as a sort of collectively produced mental weather. Media transforms experience, memory, and communication into something synthetic and external, though technological progress is rapidly integrating this external terrain into our sense of self. Books, recordings, movies, radio, television, internet, mobile phones: each of these successive innovations has penetrated deeper into daily life, mediating an ever greater proportion of our experience.

Mass media arose alongside mass production, standardizing the flow of information and producing common reference points for millions of consumers. Advertising is just one example of how this was essential for establishing the mass market, shaping the buying habits of those on the business end of the assembly line. Corporations still treat the social body as a petri dish in which tastes are cultured like bacteria, using everything from psychology to avantgarde aesthetics. The effects have spilled over into every other aspect of life; for example, politicians increasingly sell themselves like products, treating voters as consumers who want to know *what's in it for them.*

Until the end of the 20th century, mass media was essentially unidirectional, with information flowing one way and attention flowing the other. Critics generally focused on this aspect of its structure, charging that it gave a small cabal tremendous influence over society while immobilizing everyone else as spectators. In contrast, underground media explored more participatory and decentralized forms.

Participation and decentralization suddenly became mainstream with the arrival of widely accessible digital media. In many ways, the internet offered a liberating and empowering terrain for new modes of communication. The basic model was developed by academic researchers who drew their funding from the military rather than the private sector, so it was designed to be useful rather than profitable. To this day, much of the internet remains a sort of Wild West in which it's difficult to enforce traditional property laws. The ability to share content freely and directly among users has had a tremendous impact on several industries, while collaborative formats such as Wikipedia and open-source software show how easily people can meet their needs without private property. Corporations are still scrambling to figure out how to make money on the internet beyond online stores and advertising.

Yet as more and more of our lives become digitized, it's important not to take it for granted that this is always for the best. Capitalism thrives by absorbing aspects of the world that were once free and then offering access to them at a price, and this price is not always exacted in dollars.

We should be especially attentive to the ways new media are *convenient*: convenience can be a sign that the infinite possibilities of human life are being forcibly narrowed down. Indeed, these innovations are barely even optional: nowadays it's difficult to maintain friendships or get hired without a cell phone. More and more of our mental processes and social lives must pass through the mediation of technologies that map our activities and relationships for corporations as well as government intelligence. These formats also shape the content of those activities and relationships.

The networks offered by Facebook aren't new; what's new is that they seem external to us. We've always had social networks, but no one could use them to sell advertisements. Now they reappear as something we have to consult. People corresponded with old friends, taught themselves skills, and heard about public events long before email, Google, and Twitter. Of course, these technologies are extremely helpful in a world in which few of us are close with our neighbors or spend more than a few years in any location. The forms assumed by technology and daily life influence each other, making it increasingly unthinkable to uncouple them.

Another effect of digital technology is a sort of information inflation. There's more and more data in the world, coming at us faster and faster. This causes actual depreciation: for example, file-sharing and free access have driven down the online prices of movies and music. It also shortens our attention spans. Above all, though, it means that we invest this information with less and less *meaning*. We're more equipped than ever to deal with the *how* of life, but at sea as to the *why*.

As our need for and access to information increase beyond the scope of anything we could internalize, information seems to become separate from us. This is suspiciously

Consumer staring
into the void

similar to the separation required to transform workers into consumers. The information on the internet is not entirely free—computers and internet access cost money, not to mention the electrical and environmental costs of producing these and running servers all around the world. And what if corporations figure out how to charge us more for access to all these technologies once we've become totally dependent on them? If they can, not only power and knowledge but even the ability to maintain social ties will be directly contingent on wealth.

But this could be the wrong thing to watch out for. Old-money conglomerates may not be able to consolidate power in this new terrain. The ways capitalism colonizes our lives via digital technologies may not resemble the old forms of colonization.

Like any pyramid scheme, capitalism has to expand constantly, absorbing new resources and subjects. It already extends across the entire planet; the final war of colonization is being fought at the foot of the Himalayas, the very edge of the world. In theory, it should be about to collapse now that it has run out of horizons. But what if it could go on expanding *into us,* and these new technologies were like the Niña, Pinta, and Santa María landing on the continent of our own mental processes and social ties?

In this account, the internet could function as another successive layer of alienation built on the material economy. If a great deal of what is available on the internet is free of charge, this is not just because the process of colonization is not yet complete, but also because the determinant currency in the media is not dollars but *attention.* Attention functions in the information economy the same way control of material resources functions in the industrial economy. Even if attention doesn't instantly translate into income *online,* it can help secure it offline. As currencies, attention and capital behave differently, but they both serve to create power imbalances.

What is capital, really? Once you strip away the superstitions that make it seem like a force of nature, it's essentially a social construct that enables some people to amass power. Without the notion of private property, which is only "real" insofar as everyone abides by it, material resources couldn't function as capital. In this regard, property rights serve the same purpose that the notion of divine right of kings used to: both form the foundation of systems assigning sovereignty. Some people believe passionately in property rights even as those rights are used to strip them of any influence in society. It could be said that these people are *under the spell* of property.

Similarly, when an advertising agent sets out to make a meme "go viral," you could say she is trying to *cast a spell.* If attention is the currency of the media, gaining it is a way to cause people to buy literally and figuratively into a power structure. The determinant factor is not whether people agree with or approve of what they see, but to what extent it shapes their behavior.

Digital media appear to have decentralized attention, but they are also standardizing the venues through which it circulates. Beware entities that amass attention even if they never convert it into financial assets. The real power of Google and Facebook isn't in their financial holdings but in the ways they structure the flow of information.

This isn't a criticism of technology per se. The point is that it's not neutral: technology is always shaped by the structures of the society in which it is developed and applied. Most of the technologies familiar to us were shaped by the imperatives of profit, but a society based on other values would surely produce other technologies. As digital technology becomes increasingly enmeshed in the fabric of this society, the most important question is not whether to use it, but how to undermine the structures that produced it.

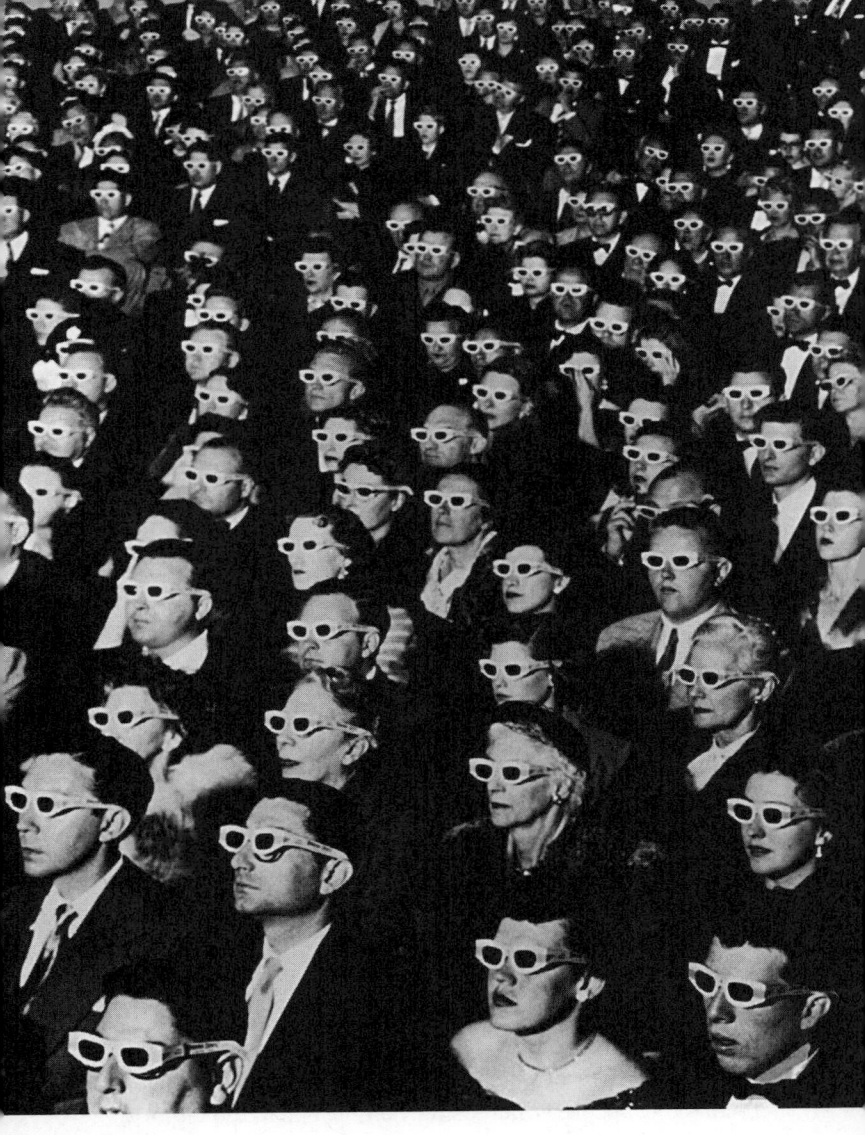

20th Century Mass Media

21ˢᵗ Century Mass Media

Bodies and Simulacra

In the Information Age, individuals are treated less as physical bodies than as assemblies of data. Whether you can get your gas turned on depends more on your credit history than how much cash you have in your wallet, let alone how cold you are; the same goes for whether you can board airplanes, cross borders, get hired, rent an apartment, or buy a house. We can be hacked, edited, even erased; identity theft has replaced kidnapping. Our flesh-and-blood existence is an inconvenient appendage to the records kept by doctors, corporations, schools, banks, and federal agents.

In this regard, the projections of ourselves that appear in social networking media don't exist outside the economy, but as extensions of it. Résumés aren't just for employers anymore—we make them for dating and for making friends, too, and our employers consult these new résumés in turn.

A facsimile of the entire world is being constructed: patents for genetic material, copyrights for ideas and artwork, call logs for conversations, test scores for knowledge, mp3s for songs. These are being mapped and coded for the convenience of the market and the forces that impose it. And this facsimile is supplanting other forms of reality: children play interactive online games rather than running around outside; ecosystems are wrecked to power internet servers.

This manifests itself in the formats we use to record data. For example, in the shift to digital technology, an infinite range of variation is translated into binary code. Converting a unique signal into ones and zeros gives the impression that everything can be reduced to a sum of interchangeable units, in accordance with the same logic that quantifies material wealth in dollars. Insofar as we must place a dollar price on the hours of our lives, human potential itself is treated as though it has an abstract exchange value.

But everything is not interchangeable; some exchanges are a one-way path. We can sell the hours of our lives for money, but we can't buy them back with the wages we receive. We can consume representations of the experiences we wish to have, but this is not the same as living them. We can construct images of ourselves, but doing so takes the place of other ways of *being ourselves*—even if we identify with our grade point averages and credit scores, we still go through life as bodies of flesh and blood.

The notion that everything is interchangeable has spread throughout our society. For example, some believe that the solution to soaring greenhouse gas emissions is to establish a market in carbon credits and offsets, in which corporations buy and sell the right to emit carbon dioxide. This policy sees individual trees as literally interchangeable; cutting down an old-growth rainforest is fine so long as someone replaces it elsewhere, even if the replacement is a homogeneous corporate tree farm on the other side of the planet.

Likewise, some argue that the transition from print to electronic media is good for the environment. But the desire to protect specific individual forests has more in common with the attachment to specific individual books than it does with the idea that whole libraries can be digitized without any loss. A database is not the same as a book collection. Anyone who doesn't get this is looking at the world through a lens of abstraction—the same way a timber company does.

An appendage of flesh on a machine of ions

Like other outmoded paradigms, old-fashioned materialism has become the province of the very rich. Fine art collecting, for example, is one of the few fields in which individual objects are still regarded as possessing nontransferable value: a Van Gogh painting is considered valuable as a unique physical object, not just as a reproducible aesthetic composition.

But it's outdated to equate greed with materialism. Avarice has become abstract, metaphysical. Greed is no longer the desire to possess the existing world, but a compulsion to reduce it to signifiers of status and control.

SEVERAL YEARS AGO I worked in a forty-two acre greenhouse complex at the heart of North America's tomato industry.

The environment inside the greenhouse was entirely computer-controlled, heated with steam and hot water from an immense system of boilers and pipes and cooled by fans and mechanized louvers. The tomato vines grew unnaturally long, sustained by complicated life-support systems. They were automatically watered by tubes, rooted in "Horticultural Rock Wool," doused in chemicals, stretched and swollen by fertilizers, strung up on strings, pruned of leaves, and pollinated by bees that lived in cardboard hives stacked here and there like miniature condominium developments. The hives inevitably emptied out as the bees succumbed to the pesticides; they were periodically replaced by new cardboard condominiums.

We used round magnetic "keys" to enter and leave the warehouse; a piercing alarm sounded whenever a door stayed open too long. Every employee was given a plastic timecard with which to swipe in and out at the beginning and end of every workday. A sign beside the time box warned us: NO PUNCH NO PAY.

We were all issued palm pilots sealed in aqua packs. We wore them on strings attached to our belts or slung over our shoulders, and as we worked we recorded everything we did on them. Every morning I entered my employee number, my task, and the greenhouse and row number. The palm pilot would start timing me; it continued until I told it I'd finished the row, or taken a break, or switched to something else. Then, if I was picking, I would enter how many crates I'd picked. Crate by crate, row by row, every minute of the day was precisely accounted for.

After work each day we lined up to place our palm pilots on metal pads in front of the office, from which the data we'd generated was automatically uploaded to some giant database. Our machines—that's what we called them, *nuestras maquinas*—then gave us an "efficiency rating" expressed as a percentage. "109," my machine would blip at the end of a particularly hard day, indicating that I'd performed 109 percent of what some English-speaker in a business suit had determined to be an acceptable day's work.

When the "machines" were first introduced, the supervisor told us that whoever had the best efficiency rating each week would get a paid day off. It's hard to convey how profoundly this threatened our culture of solidarity. In the vines, everyone moved at more or less the same pace. The faster workers slowed down to help the slower ones with their rows, and everyone emerged almost simultaneously, their crates full of tomatoes. With the threat of being sent back to Mexico hanging in the air, the last thing anyone wanted was to draw attention to himself by standing out as faster or slower than the rest.

But under the new palm pilot regime, the protective anonymity of moving at an even pace was temporarily fractured, as each worker ran himself ragged to improve his percentage while resenting the others who risked making him look bad by doing the same thing. Finally, everyone got together and refused to use the palm pilots at all. An uneasy truce reigned for a few days until the management retaliated by sending six suspected leaders back to Mexico and revoking the prize for the fastest worker. The workers who were sent home were replaced with contract workers from Jamaica—a blatant divide-and-conquer tactic. Everyone else caved in and began using the palm pilots again.

The palm pilots were so effective that we barely ever saw the English-speaking white folks in charge. Human supervision was almost irrelevant. Control was seamless and practically invisible—a corporate Human Resources department's ideal. The boss didn't have to watch us with a whip: he was hanging around our necks, he was inside our heads.

It's been a long time since I worked at the greenhouse, but I keep thinking about the palm pilots. They give me a different perspective on the technologies everybody takes for granted these days. Many of these are part of our off-the-clock lives—they really are "our" machines—but that just gives them more access to us.

Whenever my friends send text messages, I imagine duplicates appearing instantly in federal and corporate databases. When they update their online profiles, I wonder how long it will be before employers and landlords use the same system to track us, setting our wages and security deposits accordingly. What if our workplace productivity, our credit rating, how many "friends" we have, and how many hits our videos get could all be correlated into a master "efficiency rating" indicating our total economic worth? What if *nuestras maquinas* could be connected directly to the stock market so stockbrokers could buy and sell shares in real time as these ratings changed? What if we all got shares in that stock—not just financially, but also in attention and social status? Would it be possible to distinguish ourselves from our economic roles then?

Maybe I shouldn't be so suspicious. In Egypt, people just used the same technologies to coordinate a massive uprising—although as soon as it got off the ground, the government pulled the plug. Could we do something like that here, or are we too busy constructing our virtual personas? Would they pull the plug on us, too—or will they never have to?

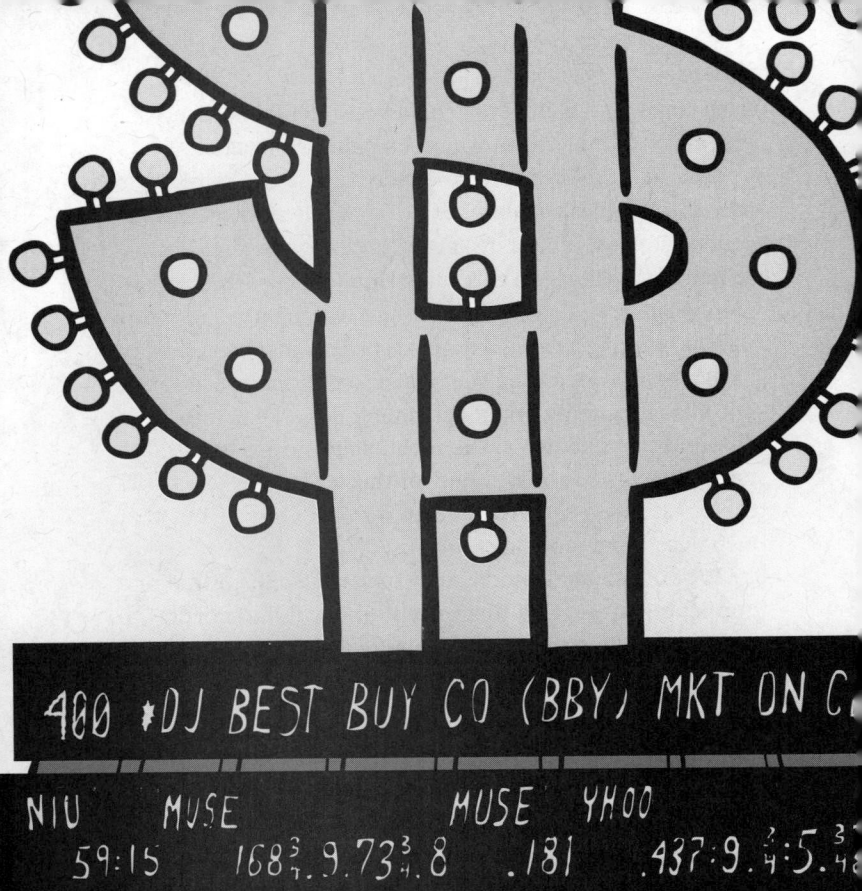

Finance

Under capitalism, *everything* ends up on the market: not just material goods and labor, but also mortgages, insurance policies, tax liens, and every other conceivable form of wealth and income. Debt itself becomes a commodity to be bought and sold, along with liability. On top of the material economy in which people actually make, buy, and sell things, another layer of capitalism appears consisting of new kinds of speculation increasingly divorced from any material point of reference.

The effects are surreal. Stock prices have become so important that corporate CEOs sacrifice long-term opportunities for short-term increases in stock value. Employees of Wall Street hedge funds troll the blogs of Midwestern farmers trying to get an edge in the futures market in agricultural products. Bona fide astrophysicists develop extremely complex strategies for investing in options contracts. Banks buy up all the tax debt in various states and turn it into securities to sell to investors. One investment firm buys collateralized debt obligations only in order to bet against them, then reaps huge profits when the economy collapses.

The dynamics of this layer of the market are so complex that not even the most influential powerbrokers can keep up with them. And yet since the 1960s, a tremendous part of economic activity has shifted from producing actual goods and services to speculating in financial markets such as the stock market and its derivatives.

Consequently, recent economic crises have originated in the speculation economy rather than the material economy. It's no longer simply a matter of corporations making more merchandise than they can sell or borrowing more than they can repay. Today, bankers, hedge funds, insurance companies, and others have spun an intricate web of financial obligations across the entire world—so when someone defaults on one obligation, investors lose faith in the other links in the web and the whole thing trembles.

The first layer of the speculation economy includes markets on which more or less straightforward assets are sold. These include *stocks,* which are shares of ownership in corporations; *commodities,* such as raw materials and agricultural goods; and *bonds,* which are essentially loans issued to corporations or government agencies. The value of these assets is relatively easy to pin down. A company has value because it owns buildings and machinery and produces a certain amount of money each quarter. Commodities have value because people need them and are willing to pay for them. Bonds have value because they represent a promise of future repayment, usually with interest.

But an additional layer of "derivatives" has been erected upon these markets. A derivative is essentially an investment that has no inherent value, but derives its value from something else. One common derivative is a *stock option,* which is essentially a contract describing a potential transaction. The purchaser pays a certain price and obtains the right to either buy or sell a given stock at a predetermined price within a certain amount of time. This option has no value in itself; its value is determined by the difference between the actual value of the stock in question and the agreed buy or sell price. For example, if an investor purchases a stock option that gives her the right to buy shares in a company for $100 per share by November, and the shares increase in value to $110 before then, then the option is worth $10 per share. On the other hand, if shares fail to break $100 by November, the investment is worthless.

The original impetus for these derivatives was to create price stability in the financial markets. If an investor owned lots of shares that were trading at $100 and was worried about a possible drop in the price, she could pay a small fee for an option that guaranteed her the right to sell the stock at $100—a form of price insurance. But as the purchaser doesn't have to own the stock in question to buy an option on it, these derivatives offer a cheap and easy way to place massive bets on price fluctuations. Stock options are only one kind of derivative; *futures* are the equivalent for commodity trading, and there are derivatives based on other assets as well.

Assets that have been standardized so they can easily be traded in volume for a predictable market price are called "securities." Stocks and bonds are two forms of securities, but there are many more. For example, a bank might buy up thousands of car loans from around the country. These loans represent a large amount of cash that is expected to flow in over time. The bank could then split this pool up into thousands of pieces, to minimize the danger posed by any one debtor defaulting, and sell small pieces to investors. Each investor would then be entitled to a small share of the future revenue generated by the loans. This process is extremely profitable to banks and is known as "securitization."

As in the securitization process, investors often make a point of spreading their funds between many different investments, so if one loses money it won't have a tremendous impact. One way to do this is to combine many investments into a pool and then sell small shares in the pool. Some mutual funds offer professional management of this kind of diversified investment.

Viewed as a whole, the speculation economy functions as a huge gambling den. Like in any casino, there are winners

and losers, and the house always comes out ahead. Broker-
age firms profit on every trade; institutional investors have
a vast advantage over individuals.

In this context, *information* is the most valuable commodity, serving as capital by enabling speculators to make

the right investments. This increases the need for cutting-edge analysts and technologies, a cost that excludes most people from competing at this level. And this information is increasingly self-referential: investors lay their bets according to corporate performance and economic forecasts, but also according to what they think others will predict. The collective psychology of participants has become one of the most determinant factors in the speculation economy, studied by a host of oracles and soothsayers.

At the upper levels of this market, an elite uses super-computers to detect minute price discrepancies and rack up profits by tremendous amounts of high-speed buying and selling. This "high-frequency trading" now accounts for the vast majority of financial market activity in the US. In this regard, artificial intelligence already runs some sectors of the economy, without consideration for common sense—witness the "flash crash" of May 2010, when the Dow Jones Industrial Average took its steepest dive in history only to recover within minutes. Here access to technology *directly* determines ability to profit: the faster the computer, the greater the advantage.

The explosion of financial speculation as an economic sector unto itself engenders a range of new dangers. The ease with which capital can flow to new investments can artificially inflate values. This creates bubbles that eventually burst, such as the dot-com boom of the turn of the century. Even the most sophisticated investors often have no idea what they're invested in or how much material wealth is actually backing it up. And all this interconnection spreads risk; although small losses can be absorbed more easily by many investors, large shocks like the financial meltdown of 2008 are felt worldwide.

The shift from production to speculation is another step in the extension of the logic of the market. It gives large-scale capitalism a foothold in every aspect of daily life: a Dutch bank may have a stake in your local diner, while part of your mortgage payment might go to a Brazilian hedge fund even though you took out your loan from the local community bank. Perhaps capitalists must come up with more and more complex abstractions in order to concentrate capital further; you can only make a certain amount of profit in the stock market, but derivatives offer investors the possibility of magnifying their gains out of all proportion to the value of the actual goods in question.

Speculation builds increasingly abstract structures of competition further and further removed from the material world. But private property and money are also *superstitions,* no more "real" than the most inflated stock price; the laws of physics are arguably inescapable, but the laws of economics are only imposed on us by collective acceptance of certain premises. Long ago, useful goods such as salt were used for currency; these were replaced by forms that were tangible but useless, such as gold and silver. At first, dollars were supposed to represent quantities of these, but eventually they were severed from any material referent other than what people accepted them to be worth. Today, even physical dollars are becoming rare: wealth is simply a matter of balance sheets, ghostly incantations exerting a sinister influence over humanity. The only thing *real* about any of this are the power imbalances that result.

The fiction of capital has produced an increasingly complex web of other fictions that have dramatic effects on those who live according to them. There's nothing inevitable about the capitalist economy; it's simply one way of organizing resources and relationships so that power concentrates in the hands of a few. It's a much more complicated way of doing this than feudalism, but also more flexible and effective. Yet a different set of criteria for how to relate to our surroundings and each other would produce a totally different world.

Investment

It used to be easy enough to distinguish capitalists from the exploited: some people owned capital, others didn't. Today speculation and credit make it very difficult to pin down exactly who makes up the capitalist class. Is it everybody who owns stock? Everybody who *profits* on it? If you own a house that is increasing in market value, does that make you a capitalist? What if you still owe the bank for most of its cost? If housing prices plummet, do you suddenly cease to be a capitalist?

A century ago, most of the US population had no investments in the stock market and few workers owned their own homes. Now that investment plans are common and loans enable more people to own real estate, many workers have become microcapitalists who associate their interests with the performance of the market even though they have very little influence within it. They spend their lives slaving away under bosses—yet when the market crashes, they hope to see their portfolio values go back up rather than the collapse of capitalism.

Until recently, after a certain number of years of labor employees were generally guaranteed a pension from their employers along with Social Security payments from the government. Nowadays, few companies offer pension plans and Social Security is regarded as unreliable. Instead of pension plans, employers often set up 401(k) plans through which their employees entrust their savings to money management companies that invest it in the stock market. To give employees an interest in their company's performance, these investment plans are often tied to the company's stock, though this dependence can put them at risk—think of the employees who lost billions of dollars when the Enron Corporation went bankrupt.

In effect, middle-class and even lower-class people are pooling their money to participate in the speculation economy alongside large-scale capitalists. When people speak about hedge funds and investment banking, they often imagine billionaires on yachts. In fact, there are comparatively few billionaires; in some ways, the big players are the institutions that manage all the 401(k) money. This creates a direct tie between "average people" and high finance, so that workers sink or swim according to the same forces as those at the top. Ironically, if workers were still receiving pensions instead of 401(k) plans, the economic crisis of 2008 would probably have been much less severe, and would have affected "Main Street" significantly less than Wall Street.

The other major factor encouraging workers to identify their interests with the market is home ownership, which functions as another form of investment. Seeking to make homes affordable for average working families is US government policy, and there may be some altruism behind this;

stocks (stŏks) *n., pl.* **1.** An instrument of punishment consisting of an adjustable wooden structure with holes for securing a person's feet and hands, in which criminals were locked and exposed to public ridicule or assault. **2.** The shares of a particular company, type of company, or industry: *blue-chip stocks.*

bonds (bŏndz) *n., pl.* **1.** Physical restraints used to hold someone or something prisoner, esp. ropes or chains. **2.** Certificates issued by a government or a public company promising to repay borrowed money at a fixed rate of interest at a specified time.

but economists explain frankly that it helps create a docile workforce. Mortgages typically last 15 to 30 years—the length of a career.

Before the Second World War, credit was hard to come by and hardly anyone had the cash to buy a house up front. After the war, the government started guaranteeing loans through Fannie Mae and Freddie Mac, government-sponsored private institutions that buy almost all mortgages in the country so that smaller banks won't be putting themselves at risk by making loans to people who may default on them. This made it much easier for middle-class and working-class families to become homeowners.

In a thriving market, home ownership is a form of microcapitalism. A homeowner stands to profit as long as the market value of her house increases faster than the interest on the mortgage. For example, let's say someone takes out a high-interest loan and buys a house for $200,000. If the house appreciates to $220,000, she comes out ahead even if she had only been able to pay off the interest on the loan, provided that the interest was less than $20,000. What's more, the additional $20,000 value of the house makes her less of a credit risk, so she can take out a new loan at a lower interest rate to replace the old one. Presto, she's just advanced to a better position in the economy.

So homeowners have a variety of reasons to want their homes to increase in value, which is most likely to happen

when the market is running smoothly. This spreads a capitalist mentality to everyone: rather than escaping from work, workers aspire to obtain capital of their own, however humble. Once you own something, you have something to lose; you become invested in the property system and its premises. Fighting the injustices of the system means putting what you own at risk—so the more you own, the less incentive you have to stir things up. This dynamic can play out even when you don't actually *own* anything except investments that *might* pay off.

This explains why people went in for the sub-prime loans that set off the financial crisis of 2008 when too many debtors defaulted on them. As long as the value of your home increases over time, it doesn't matter how bad the loan you got for it was—you can simply refinance at better terms. But the majority of the property on the market can't increase in value *indefinitely*. This strategy of investing in real estate is basically a pyramid scheme, in that those who get into the market later produce the wealth of those already involved. It works out well as long as more people are getting into it and the value of real estate is increasing, but sooner or later the bubble is bound to burst. In this sense, the foreclosures of the past few years are punishment for poor people trying to speculate the way rich people do.

Money makes money; that's the first law of capitalism. Therefore it makes perfectly good sense to borrow money with which to make money, at least if you think you can earn more with it than you'll have to pay in interest. This is what entrepreneurs are doing when they take out start-up loans; corporations do the same thing by issuing bonds, and hedge funds do this by borrowing money with which to buy stocks. But the money to pay off these loans has to come from somewhere, and if everyone's gambling on coming out ahead some are bound to lose big sooner or later.

The premise of the neoliberal era leading up to the 2008 crash was that the market could expand forever. History revealed this to be a pipe dream. For a pyramid scheme to expand indefinitely, there have to be an infinite supply of resources and an infinite number of potential participants. Capitalism can produce more efficient technologies, but the raw materials of this earth are limited, and there may be limits to how much profit can be squeezed out of human beings. More to the point—even if the Dow Jones Industrial Average could increase indefinitely, everyone can't become wealthier *relative to everyone else*. Every time one person gains greater financial leverage in proportion to the total wealth of society, others lose leverage, proportionately speaking. Capitalism tends to concentrate wealth in fewer and fewer hands, which means a lot of people end up on the losing end of this equation. Many homeowners found this out the hard way when their real estate investments plummeted while the banks continued profiting off them.

Loaning money to aspiring capitalists is good business. The only risk is that if too many of them can't repay their loans, the pyramid scheme collapses, bringing down creditors and debtors alike. Even in this situation, however, the poor still pay the way for the rich. The ones at the top of the pyramid have governments to bail them out—with tax money taken from those at the bottom.

Debt

*"The replacement for the wage was debt—money one
could spend, but that had to paid back, literally binding
the once-rebellious poor to the infinite continuation of
capitalism. Debt is the perfect commodity, and the future
itself became the new market; the financial market was
born, ushering in the era of postmodernism."*
– Anonymous, *Introduction to the Apocalypse*

Credit serves several crucial roles in capitalism. It offers those
who have money a way to profit on it simply by loaning it
out and charging interest. It expands the market, enabling
capitalists to go on selling things even after consumers'
pockets are empty. It offers the prospect of economic mobility,
equipping people to try their luck as entrepreneurs or investors—channeling their ambitions to improve their lives into
the economy rather than into contesting it. Finally, it makes
it possible for low-income workers to partake in the lifestyles
of the wealthy, buying houses and cars and college degrees.
This serves to make people see themselves as middle class
even as they are fleeced by banks and credit card companies.

Consumer credit offered a solution for the economic
turmoil of the early 20th century. Without credit, mass production could only enable the capitalist class to make as
much money from workers as it paid them. Credit enables
capitalists to colonize the future as well as the present, accumulating long-term obligations as well as immediate profit.

For production to go smoothly, workers have to suspend their desires and suppress spontaneous impulses; to maximize sales, they have to buy impulsively and seek instant gratification. Hence, to optimize profit, capitalists must impose a sort of split personality disorder on the general public. Lending functions on both sides of this equation. On the consumption side, it offers workers a taste of the standard of living they envy in their bosses, permitting them to indulge in luxuries beyond their means. In the workplace, the resulting debt forces them to *discipline themselves*—instead of aspiring to escape servitude, they aspire to pay for what they already "own."

This is not always even possible. Over the past decade, total household debt in the US has grown significantly greater than annual household income. Many among the poor, precarious, and unemployed have little hope of ever achieving solvency.

In the "company towns" of the old days, workers bought the tools and goods they needed on credit, then were trapped indefinitely working to pay off their debts. Today this story outrages people—but what if the same scam were perpetrated by a *class* rather than a single corporation? Student loans ensnare young workers more effectively than any general store could have. Likewise, the only difference between debt and old-fashioned indentured servitude is that now the servitude is owed to the economy in general rather than a particular individual or institution.

If we look at debt as a form of *obligation,* it starts to sound suspiciously familiar. Some are born with little, and can only get what they need on the condition that they pledge themselves to service; others start out with plenty and are so generous as to loan some of it to the needy in return for this pledge. This is simply a new incarnation of the duty the poor have owed the rich since feudal times, updated to appear voluntary.

Many fortunes literally consist of the debts of the poor. Debt is the perfect commodity, as interest makes it accrue value on its own ahead of inflation—hence its attractiveness to banks and investors. But if the poor keep getting poorer, it might turn out to be a risky investment. For debt to retain its value, there must be no chance of social change; the future must remain an eternally frozen version of the present. Collection agencies force this present on debtors, while police form the front lines against the future—witness the SWAT teams that remove foreclosure resisters from their homes.

Yet there aren't enough SWAT teams to empty every foreclosed house. When enough debtors start standing up for themselves, taking and defending what they need in defiance of their creditors, the frozen future will begin to crack and thaw. There's no shame in bankruptcy in a bankrupt system.

We're all sharecroppers owing the company store.

Banking

When an employee makes a little money and wants to keep it somewhere, she puts it in a bank account. This is considered safer than just keeping it under the mattress. In the US, bank accounts are federally insured, so there's little danger that the customer won't get it back. The real risk lies in what the banks do with all this wealth; it's ironic that even when the exploited have some money of their own, they entrust it to capitalists so the latter can go on accruing profit.

In effect, the customer is loaning money to the bank, the same way banks loan money to other customers. The bank's business plan is to borrow money as cheaply as possible and sell loans for as much as possible, profiting on the difference in interest rates; they have to make enough in the process to cover their operating expenses and the occasional loan default. Of course, just as the depositor's balance is government-insured, the government protects banks against defaulters by enforcing their right to foreclose on "collateral assets"—such as people's homes—and often by buying mortgages outright as well. This ensures that when something goes awry the cost comes out of taxpayers' pockets, so the banks can go on profiting.

Banks don't just take money from depositors; money itself is a commodity, and banks get it wherever it's cheapest. Today, the government loans money to banks for an unprecedented 0% interest—sometimes less—and the regulations that prohibited banks from selling stocks and bonds have been eliminated. If it's more profitable for a bank to participate in the financial market than to issue loans, it will focus on the former. Banks are willing to pay interest for large deposits from customers, but those with less money have to accept low interest rates or even pay the bank to keep and use their money. This is emblematic of how capital works, "naturally" flowing from low concentrations to high concentrations.

The practice of loaning out borrowed money has the uncanny effect of "multiplying" the amount of money available to a bank. Imagine that a person deposits $100 in a bank, and the bank loans that money to another person who uses it to buy goods from the first person. The first person deposits that additional $100, and the bank loans it out again to someone else who also uses it to make a purchase from the original account holder. This process can occur many times, increasing the assets of the bank by multiplying others' obligations to it.

The only problem is that these loans have to come back in eventually or else the whole system collapses—and as the poorest get the highest interest rates, they're under the most pressure to come up with money as if out of thin air. This is one of the reasons capitalism has to go on expanding indefinitely to avoid crisis. The position of banks is actually less precarious than it sounds—between charging interest and receiving government bailouts, they usually do quite well for themselves even during financial meltdowns.

When banks run low on cash, they borrow money from the government's federal reserve banks. Together these banks constitute the US central bank, providing the government with a mechanism for controlling the growth of the economy by dictating the interest rates on loans to other banks.

Of course, the money from the federal reserve banks has to come from somewhere, too. The US government has a few different ways of producing funds for this. It can raise taxes. It can eliminate social services, as many European governments are doing right now. It can sell bonds, essentially taking out loans from private investors. Finally, it can print more money. In the virtual era, this simply means jacking up the numbers on a balance sheet.

So money, the cause of so much anguished yearning and pursuit, is simply made up, albeit under very specific conditions. Just as the Church invented the soul to establish its power and kings propagated the notion of duty, one might say that money is generated in order to *create debt*. All of these are ways to structure a social system based on obligation.

Inside the logic of this system, a thousand pressures combine to force the participants to be absolutely ruthless; yet the system itself is hardly necessary. Debtors' prison was finally abolished because even legislators were forced to agree that a bank shouldn't be able to foreclose

on someone's freedom. If we want access to housing and other necessities to be determined by anything other than what makes money for banks, we have to disconnect them from the banking system as well.

But barbaric and precarious as it is, it's possible that capitalism will somehow perpetuate itself indefinitely, each risk propelling it forward, each crisis renewing it. The real danger is not that the system will collapse, but that it might go on inflicting the unsustainable costs of its operation upon us forever.

The 2008 Financial Crisis!

CAUTION: TECHNICAL DETAILS!

The financial crisis of 2008 was the logical conclusion of free market development of the financial sector—itself the logical result of the incentives of capitalist competition. In that sense, the economic downturn demonstrates the inherent instability of capitalism itself.

The story of the collapse starts and ends in the real estate market. Until a few decades ago, community banks would issue loans to locals. These banks didn't have a tremendous amount of money to work with, so issuing mortgages was a comparatively big risk for them; they had to make sure their borrowers could afford the loans. But since they were doing business on such a small scale, bankers could develop relationships with their clients in order to make prudent decisions about whom to issue loans to. This worked smoothly enough for several decades.

In the late 1980s, investment bankers got to thinking about this situation. Investors wanted a way to invest in mortgages across the country, so the bankers designed a system whereby they could *securitize* home mortgages. Banks would buy up many mortgages and pool them together, then sell chunks of the pool to investors. One example of this kind of security is called a Collateralized Debt Obligation (CDO). Ratings agencies—companies that are paid to assess the risk involved with different investments—proclaimed that CDOs were very safe, giving them their highest grade: AAA.

For the first decade or so, the growth of the CDO market was slow. This changed around the turn of the century. Due to government policies, big investors were having a hard time finding profitable places to put their money. It turned out that CDOs offered interest rates up to 3% higher than other similarly graded investments. Money started pouring into the market. In 2004, about $20 billion in new CDOs were issued; three years later this had ballooned to $180 billion.

Banks such as Countrywide Financial Services welcomed this demand for CDOs and changed their business models to accommodate it. Instead of issuing and holding onto mortgages for 15 or 20 years, they started making loans and then selling them almost immediately to Wall Street investors. As demand for CDOs peaked, banks were scrambling to cash in.

The demand for investments in mortgages created an incentive for banks to make loans to people who had no hope of ever paying them off.

Soon they ran out of borrowers with good credit. Instead of curtailing their activities, however, banks began issuing "subprime" loans to borrowers who would be less likely to be able to pay them off. Because of the risk, subprime loans imposed much harsher terms on borrowers; even though interest rates usually started low, they often skyrocketed over time. The market for these loans produced a culture of fraud: bankers would convince customers that they could afford loans they could never repay, then help them fraudulently fill out paperwork to get them.

For consumers, this seemed like a dream come true at first. People who had previously had little hope of ever owning a home could suddenly get loans. True, the terms were very bad, but all these new buyers were sending the price of homes through the roof. As long as home prices continued to increase, new home-buyers could purchase homes with subprime loans, then refinance into better loans a few years later when their home values had increased. In short, the entire banking establishment was selling a pyramid scheme.

As banks pooled their subprime loans to sell as CDOs, some Wall Street investors started to look at their investment portfolios. They saw that they owned a lot of these CDOs and that the loans backing them were less and less likely to be repaid. To hedge their positions, they turned to insurance companies, which created policies called Credit Default Swaps (CDSs). These are derivatives based on CDOs that pay the holder if the CDO goes bad. For example, if an

When people couldn't repay these loans, the house of cards collapsed, bringing down banks, investors, and real estate prices too.

investor bought a CDO from a bank, she could also buy a credit default swap from the insurance company covering that CDO; the insurance company would pay her if the bank was unable to pay what it had guaranteed in the CDO.

But, just like a stock option, you didn't actually have to own a CDO to buy the swap that was based on it—so investors just started trading the CDSs. Pretty soon the size of the CDS market exploded, reaching several hundred times the value of the CDO market—meaning that for every dollar of debt that went unpaid, CDS investors would have to pay out several hundred dollars. The system was incredibly unstable: the market only had to start going downhill a little bit to cause huge effects.

Things started to unravel as early as 2007. More and more struggling homeowners were defaulting on their mortgages; as a result, investors began backing away from CDOs and other mortgage-backed securities. Many investment analysts downgraded their ratings for these products; demand for them soon dried up entirely.

As it became more difficult to sell mortgage-backed securities, banks like Countrywide Financial developed serious problems. These banks depended on re-selling these securities in order to finance their operations; once the market for CDOs and similar assets dried up, they became insolvent. Many went into bankruptcy or, as in the case of Countrywide, were bought out by larger banks for pennies on the dollar.

Next, a huge Wall Street financial services company called Lehman Brothers was forced into bankruptcy due to its investment in subprime mortgages. The collapse of Lehman Brothers was like a shot heard around the world. Lehman had been a respected pillar of the investment world for over a hundred years; if they could implode, any company could.

Fear spread through Wall Street. Suddenly, anyone with investments in the mortgage market became suspect. AIG, a huge insurance firm, had issued credit default swaps insuring over $440 billion worth of CDOs. Even though AIG had guaranteed that it would pay if these CDOs went bad, the company had never been required to keep enough cash on hand to pay off these obligations. But as the subprime mortgage crisis spread, analysts recognized the huge risk in AIG's policies and lowered the company's credit rating.

The lower credit rating meant that AIG had to put up a percentage of all the money it had promised through CDS sales. Of course, it had no way to come up with this kind of cash. After Lehman brothers, the government had decided that allowing these huge companies to go into bankruptcy caused too many problems in the economy, so it stepped in with bailout money. Around this time a number of other institutions such as Fannie Mae, Freddie Mac, Goldman Sachs, and Morgan Stanley all received similar bailouts.

The credit market collapsed. No one knew how much this affected any particular company because the investments were so widespread and complicated. For example, if CitiBank had bought a Credit Default Swap from AIG and then sold one to Merrill Lynch, it might seem that it was not at risk. But if Merrill Lynch came asking for its money and AIG couldn't pay out, then suddenly CitiBank would be responsible for that debt. Faith in the financial market evaporated; almost overnight it became impossible for companies to get loans for practically anything.

This lack of credit quickly trickled down to consumers, sending the real estate market into a nose dive. As credit became less available, demand for houses plummeted and home prices fell through the floor. Suddenly thousands upon thousands of homeowners owed more for their homes than they were worth; this increased defaults. More defaults meant more problems in the financial markets, which meant less credit, lower home prices, and more defaults. It was a downward spiral.

The stock market plunged. The value of stocks declined as much as 50%. Combined with the credit crunch, this sent companies into a panic. They began laying off employees by the thousand. Many laid-off employees could no longer afford their mortgages, so they defaulted. This further worsened the financial crisis, which reduced credit availability, which caused more layoffs. Another vicious spiral. At the bottom of the crisis, over 10% of US citizens were out of work—a great deal more if you include those who gave up looking for jobs.

The US government repeatedly attempted to revive the economy, infusing vast sums into the same financial sectors that caused the crash in the first place. Instead of feeding all this free cash into the US economy, banks and other large corporations hoarded it or put it into overseas investments. So by 2010 corporations were posting huge profits again; stock market indexes soared, some almost doubling from their lows in 2009. All this while unemployment remained around 10%, much higher in some places, and home prices continued to drop.

The bankers who set out to cash in by ripping off home-buyers were simply obeying the imperatives of financial capitalism—those who didn't were replaced by less scrupu-lous competitors. The same goes for the homebuyers who took out loans beyond their means and the insurers whose guarantees only made things worse. All of them were acting rationally within the capitalist framework. The problem was that the framework itself is senseless.

In 2008, at the height of the crisis, capitalism was shaken to its foundations. The system had proven that it didn't work.

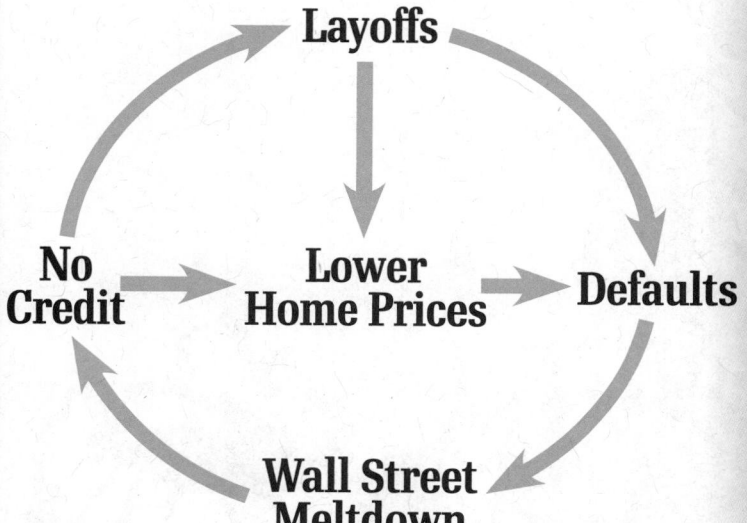

For the first time in generations, we saw the ones at the top shiver as they realized that the pyramid was a house of cards. One might expect fundamental change in response to such a catastrophe—at the very least, an effort to redistribute wealth similar to the New Deal with which Roosevelt's government sought to counteract the Great Depression.

Instead we've seen the opposite. The capitalists at the top are gambling that they don't need the US middle class anymore—neither as employees nor as consumers. They had already moved most of their production jobs overseas. Now they're betting on the emergence of a middle class in China to consume the goods they produce. In the future, if you're not part of the capitalist class in the US, you'll serve that class on the cheap, or be out of a job.

Taxation

As a variant of flat-out extortion, taxation is among the oldest methods of financial gain. The compulsory nature of taxation identifies it with the practice of organized crime syndicates demanding protection money. Of course, governments make the laws, so they can make it a crime *not* to pay.

One justification for government is that it is a means of pooling resources to serve the greater good. But monarchies weren't invented as a way to provide for the needs of the general public! Historically, governments have only provided for the needs of the public *incidentally,* in order to pacify restless subjects; for the most part, they've focused on accumulating wealth for themselves. The state needs a steady flow of capital to maintain power, not to practice philanthropy.

Nowadays, the greatest accumulation of wealth takes place in the private sector rather than through the state apparatus, but the state is still necessary to oversee the market and preserve the imbalances it creates. For evidence, we need only look at how taxes are spent. The greatest part of the US federal budget goes to funding military and internal security. This is consistent with the way organized crime works: *you pay for your own extortion.* And we're not just paying for our own—our tax dollars fund the domination of exploited peoples around the world. In return, we enjoy the privileges of citizenship in the world's foremost superpower, but we also earn the animosity of everyone who lives under a Western-supported military regime.

Whatever politicians say about the necessity of austerity measures or the inviolability of the free market, the military and the police will always be publicly funded. Private security corporations, too, derive much of their income from the government. Imagine how much poverty could be alleviated with the hundreds of billions of dollars spent every year to protect the structures that *cause* poverty. Meanwhile, welfare programs and social services are being steadily cut, and this will continue until popular outcry becomes too fierce to be controlled by state repression. In this light, we can see why capitalists consider military power a better *investment* than social programs.

This is just one aspect of the role taxation plays in capitalism. Some taxes, such as sales tax, weigh disproportionately heavily on the poor. But even when they pay more, the wealthy get a much higher return on their taxes, receiving them back in the form of corporate subsidies and government funding for a wide range of projects advancing their interests. So taxation goes beyond mere extortion: like profit, it is a means of redistributing wealth up the pyramid on an ongoing basis.

In the age of bank bailouts, governments have become increasingly brazen about intervening to socialize liability and privatize profit. In order to bolster the economy, the government backs banks and buys up mortgages, enabling private capitalists to make millions speculating on the financial market. When these schemes don't pan out, the general public has to pay for it. Between government and business, they've got us coming and going.

Inheritance

Property still passes from one generation to the next the way kingship once did. Wealth couldn't remain so disproportionately distributed if it weren't concentrated across generations. Self-described capitalists often claim that they've earned everything they own, but it's never been a fair competition.

Inheritance precedes capitalism by thousands of years as a method for maintaining inequality. It's one of the oldest institutions of patriarchy; its origins are probably intertwined with the invention of private property. Marriage is one of several state-sanctioned institutions that contribute to the consolidation of property via inheritance. In debates about whether to legalize same-sex marriage, the issue is generally framed as cultural or religious, when in fact it's also economic.

In feudal Europe, when every landowner was a sort of petty prince, the oldest son would inherit the whole estate, lest it be split into smaller territories that could be easily conquered by neighbors. This forced younger siblings of wealthy birth to pursue careers in government, business, the Church, and the military, later including the colonization of overseas continents. Over time, these institutions came to determine the flow of capital as much as inheritance. But this simply means there are more ways of producing and deepening inequalities, all of which tend to reinforce each other.

Money and property are not the only things people inherit. Wealthy families pass on social skills and networks, accents and vocabularies, influential family names, and relationships with institutions—a college that receives sizable donations is more likely to admit the offspring of alumni, however dumb they are. Just as wealthy white children can inherit all these advantages and white privilege besides, African-Americans inherit the long-term effects of slavery and segregation, of their ancestors being terrorized and dispossessed and their parents struggling to compete in a racist society. The same goes for the children of indigenous people, of refugees and illegal immigrants, of all the exploited and excluded.

It's not surprising that parents want to do everything they can to provide for their children. The question is whether the best way to do this is by reproducing a system that distributes wealth so unevenly. Bequeathing their riches to the next generation, the wealthy also pass on the danger that others will win these riches. They leave their heirs a world in which everyone has to scramble to compete or face certain poverty—a world of *work*.

Research and Development

Optimists have always promised that technological development was going to unite humanity and put an end to strife and want. Antoine de Saint-Exupéry, for example, wrote beautifully about how the airplane would eliminate national conflicts and create a brotherhood of man—shortly before airplanes were used to decimate most of Europe and drop atomic bombs on Japan.

Progress itself is no panacea. Capitalism drives certain kinds of innovation faster than they have occurred under any other social system, but only to its own ends. Technologies incarnate the social and economic relations that give rise to them: in a society headed for disaster, better technology will just get us there faster.

We already possess the means to eliminate most of the hardships facing humanity, but the forces that structure our society prevent us from doing so. The same incentives that drive drug companies to develop medicines discourage them from sharing the results with the poor. Indeed, many of the hardships people face now stem from the absurd uses to which our technologies are put. We don't need innovations in technology, now, but in social structure.

From military and corporate research programs to the academic inquiries they direct, the production of knowledge is governed by the state and the market. Investigation as an end in itself—such as the NASA space program—is always driven by a hidden agenda, such as the pursuit of new weapons technology. Even when they're overseen by state organizations, the processes by which new technologies are generated are hardly "democratic"—though these often have more impact on society than any political policy could.

The specialists who carry out this development don't have bad intentions. By and large, they're motivated by curiosity, desire to utilize their talents, and aspirations to help others. But the only way they can obtain the resources and opportunities they need is to accept the direction of institutions pursuing profit or power. A few years of writing grant applications will cure anyone of idealism. How many engineers and computer programmers set out to offer something to society and end up working for the Navy?

To keep this arrangement stable, researchers are insulated from the effects of their research. Pioneers in artificial intelligence don't get bombed by killer drones in Pakistan. When the development of knowledge is separated from its application, ethical considerations become abstract. The pursuit of knowledge comes to be seen as a universal good that trumps the welfare of individual living creatures—not just in the vivisection lab but in society at large.

Ironically, under capitalism, research relies on an intellectual commons, yet produces private property. People are cleverest when they share information and ideas; today's corporations struggle to maximize collaboration while monopolizing access to the results. The ideal corporate product would be produced by the unpaid labor of the whole human race, yet only available through a single distributor. The vast majority of the work that goes into developing any patented innovation takes place long before its legally recognized inventor gets involved. Patents and intellectual property rights can reward the first one to claim a breakthrough, but they also inhibit the circulation of information and ideas.

Indeed, one of the primary functions of corporate research is to patent and suppress innovations that might disrupt

on earth as it
is in heaven

current business models. In industries in which the means of production are monopolized by a few corporations, small inventors simply can't compete, however clever their ideas are. This system isn't the most effective way to produce *knowledge*, but it is the most efficient means of turning it into *capital*.

So research serves the accumulation of capital and serves as capital itself; it also discovers new forms capital can assume. Corporations can now patent genetically engineered organisms and the use of genetic information. Our own biology has become a new territory to exploit—offering a new vista for accumulation when nearly everything we once held in common has been privatized.

Without the imperatives of capitalism, would we have invented terminator seeds or other forms of planned obsolescence? Would we focus more resources on producing technologies that cause cancer than on finding ways to cure it? Without those imperatives, what else might we create?

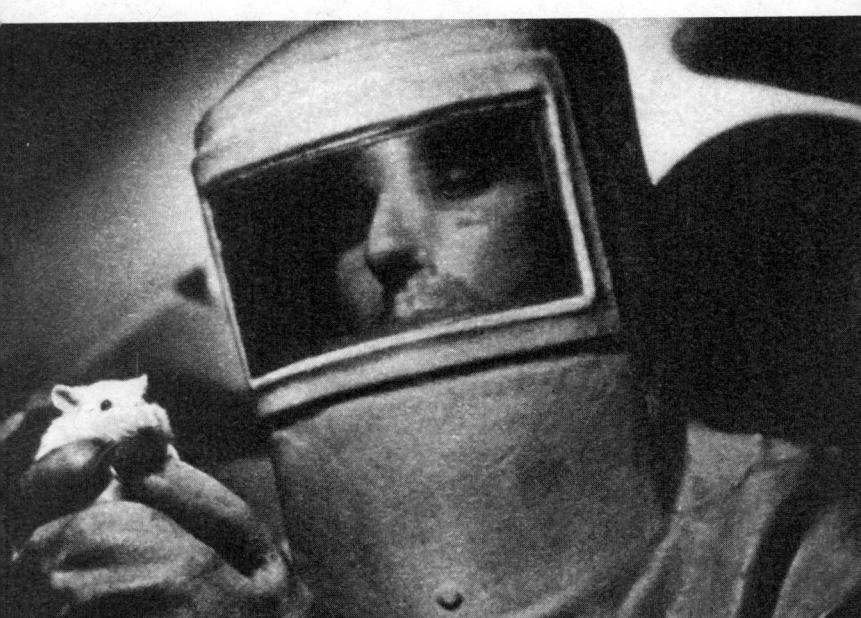

Medicine

What's more valuable than health? One of the most persua-
sive justifications for capitalism is the advancements it has
produced in medical science. And yet no previous society
distributed access to medical knowledge and treatment
as unequally as ours does. A heart transplant is a mixed
blessing when it costs you an arm and a leg!

Our bodies didn't always seem so alien to us. Once upon
a time, medicines literally grew on trees, and in every family there was someone who knew how to use them. From
the witch burnings of the Inquisition to the efforts of the
American Medical Association to limit the number of health
practitioners, centuries of deliberate assaults on traditional
healing have reduced us to helpless dependence on an elite
class of doctors. These assaults parallel the colonization of
the "New World" as a means of forcibly creating new markets.

Today our relationships with our bodies are mediated
through strangers; our bodies still send us messages, but
we are illiterate or deaf, trusting instead to nutritionists,
periodontists, gynecologists, and specialists in several
dozen other fields. We've gone beyond mind-body dualism to
divide ourselves into countless discrete parts and systems,
all of which we experience as foreign entities. Even our
own minds seem beyond our ken, putting us at the mercy
of psychiatrists, psychologists, and therapists.

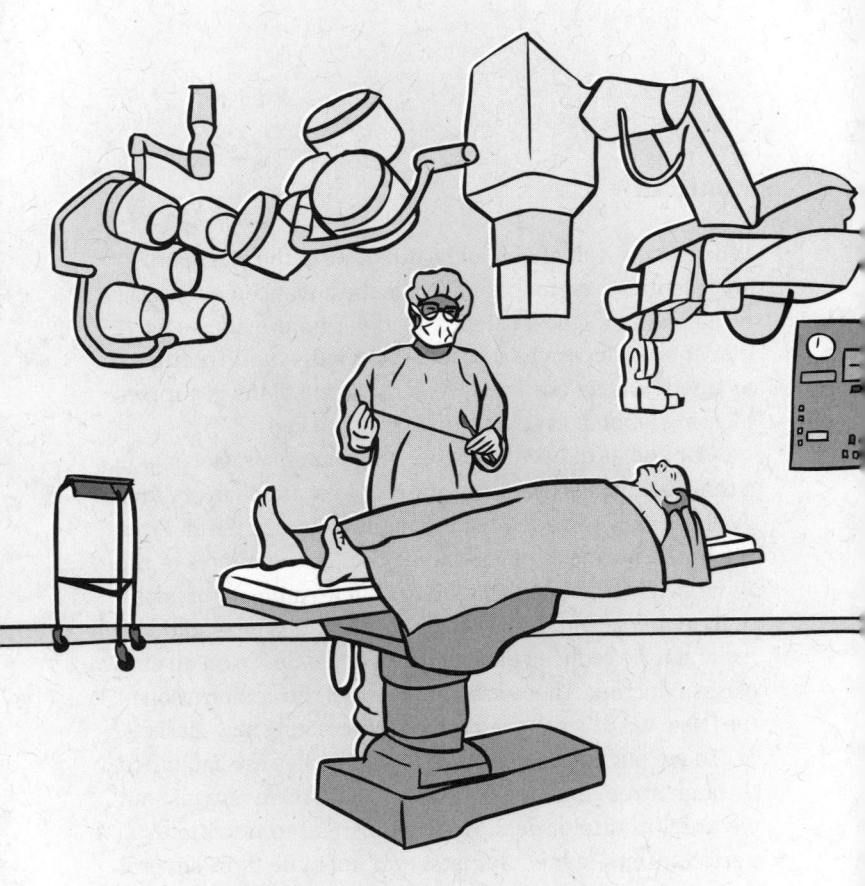

This is not to say oncologists and toxicologists aren't peddling a useful skill—they are, especially in such a polluted world. The point of all this specialization is to heal us, but principally as a way of making money, and that agenda promotes certain forms of health care over others.

For example, there is very little incentive for research into preventive medicine beyond what it takes to prevent epidemics and keep people fit for work. The medical industry makes up such a large part of the economy that if people stopped getting injured and ill it would precipitate a major crisis. On the other hand, the dangers of modern work and consumption offer lucrative business opportunities; Durham, North Carolina used to be a center of tobacco production, but now it bills itself as "The City of Medicine." Like planned obsolescence, iatrogenic illnesses—illnesses caused by the medical industry—are actually *advantageous* from a business perspective so long as they don't give one's competitors an edge. If we categorize illnesses produced by *all* types of industry as iatrogenic, the medical industry starts to look like a sort of protection racket—with the insurance industry built on top of it as *another* protection racket.

As capitalism extends further into every aspect of our lives, health is increasingly determined by the distribution of capital, and not only as a result of hospital bills. Until a few generations ago, *all* food was organic; now this is an additional selling point, and an expensive one. Health food co-ops in wealthy suburbs offer the latest fads in nutrition while other neighborhoods don't even have grocery stores, only corner stores. This mirrors the production process, in which migrant workers are exposed to pesticides while their bosses sit in orthopedic chairs.

So long as they aren't equipped to treat the social and economic causes of illness, doctors—for all their good intentions—can only treat individual pathology. In a consumption-oriented society, this largely means prescribing products.

The relationship between doctor and patient has become almost incidental to the medical profession compared to what happens in laboratories. Drug companies determine what is studied, how the findings are used, and who gets access to the results. In this context, doctors often function as little more than over-educated drug dealers.

This promotes a consumer relationship to health and a push-button attitude to our bodies. In some circles nowadays it seems like almost *everybody* is on medication—the range of treatable conditions among the middle class keeps expanding even as the afflictions of the underclass go untreated. However beneficial or harmful the effects of individual prescription products may be, they all perform a social role as well, normalizing this consumer relationship and the estrangements on which it is founded.

According to the logic of pure capitalism, the excluded should only receive health care when it is necessary to subdue them, while the exploited should receive it in ways tailored to maximize their consumption and productivity. The US is already close to this ideal, to the good fortune of rapacious insurance companies, while European governments are hastening to disassemble their social support structures. In prisons and psychiatric wards, some inmates already experience "medical treatment" chiefly as a pretext for intervention and coercion. Meanwhile, Ritalin, Prozac, Xanax, Paxil, and lithium serve the same functions as caffeine and energy drinks, greasing the wheels of the economy. The two situations are not so different: they're both ways to keep people *well-adjusted* in a dysfunctional society.

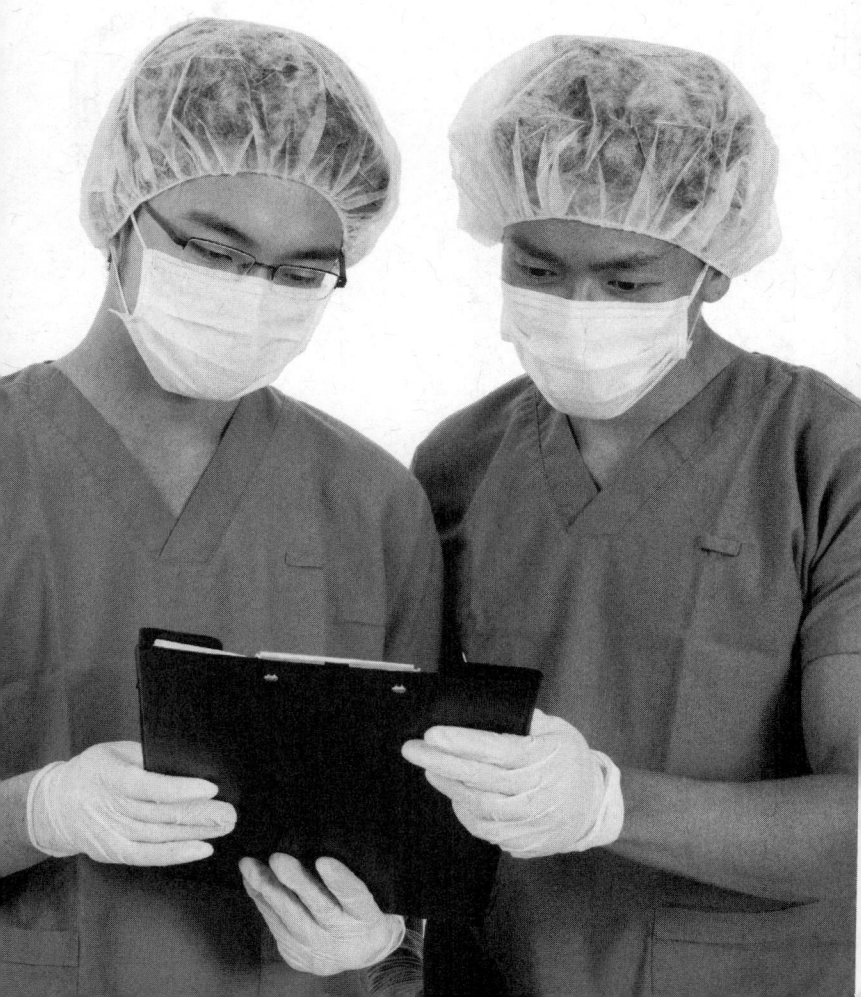

– *Do you think he'll make it?*

– *I don't know, how much is he worth?*

Identification

> "The individual deprived of meaning chooses to take
> the final leap into meaninglessness by identifying
> with the very process that deprives him. He becomes
> We, the exploited identifying with the exploiter. Hence-
> forth his powers are Our powers, the powers of the
> ensemble, the powers of the alliance of workers with
> their own bosses known as the Developed Nation."
> – Fredy Perlman

We don't identify with our own impoverished lives—these
can't be ours. We displace our aspirations, our selfhood, onto
surrogates: onto the representatives, as if by coincidence,
of those who rule and profit at our expense.

The spectator identifies with the protagonist of the movie,
the reader with the subject of the biography, the voter with
the political candidate, the shopper with the model in the
advertisement. The sports fan triumphs through his team;
the worshipper wields absolute power through her deity;
the *nobody* lives vicariously through the celebrity with a
mixture of adulation and resentment. Mopping the floor
with the radio on after close, the cashier sings along with
pop stars bragging about how much cash they make.

And the worker identifies with the capitalist. He too has
private property to defend against freeloaders—or at least
he might someday! In the free market he is a *potential* capi-

talist; shouldn't he protect his potential interests? Thanks to credit lines, practically everyone is middle class, or can try to appear to be. Who wants to admit to losing the class war when everybody else seems to be coming out ahead?

Similarly, students working low-paying jobs don't see themselves as low-paid workers, imagining that brighter prospects await them after graduation. Thus a whole class never identifies with its role or demands better treatment: if you're convinced you're on your way to a higher position on the pyramid, you *don't want* those who will be beneath you to have it better.

Nationalism and patriotism are extreme cases of this projected identification in which subjects conflate their own interests with those of their rulers. Beware the first person plural! "We have the highest standard of living in human history," brags the economist to a readership who does not share it; "The time has come to risk our lives to defend our freedom," intones the president who will never set foot on a battlefield. If a foreign army invaded the country, cut down all the trees, poisoned the rivers, and forced children to grow up dispossessed and ashamed, who wouldn't take up arms to drive them out? Yet how many people hire themselves out as willing accomplices when domestic businessmen do the same thing?

Practically all the forms of identity we know downplay differences within one category in order to emphasize the differences between categories. All categories thus tend to obscure internal power imbalances and conflicts, even as they highlight external ones. Can we imagine a togetherness that isn't founded on gross generalizations, conceptualizing ourselves as unique individuals who still stand to gain from looking out for one another? Can we identify with *each other* rather than with categories or masters?

Actually, I'm a musician.

EVERY MORNING AT HALF PAST FIVE my clock radio erupts into the newscast. Usually I'm already awake. When this first started happening, I resented that the alarm had taught me so well I almost didn't need it. Then I started to think of it ironically as a life coach encouraging me to tackle the day ahead. Now my five minutes each morning simply confirm that my body has slept enough and is fully recharged.

I'm a janitor. I never thought I'd say that. When I was a kid, I was determined to lead a life of adventure. I finished high school and signed up for an exchange program that would take me to Norway. When I told my father about it, he was furious.

"What about your *job?*" He was talking about factory job I had held for only a few months that summer.

"I'll quit," I promised. He looked confused.

"But you'll be union in six months!" At the time, I thought he was trying to kill me. The next month I left for Trondheim.

It's been almost thirty years since then. Somehow life brought me back home. I'm getting dressed for another shift cleaning at the state university. I've only been at this a few years now. The pay is decent and the union doubles my wages in benefits. I live in a small house in a working-class neighborhood; my children are grown and most of my debt is behind me. When I left home as a kid I thought my dad was insane.

I can't say I love the work environment. The students are messy and always look past me. The professors are slobs, convinced that their hard work has earned them the right not to pick up after themselves. If it weren't for the bill that comes in the mail, I'd forget I'm in a union. Most of my coworkers are grouchy white guys who hate women, and I'm usually the only woman around. I have to put up with racist slurs and misogyny.

A good janitor's work is invisible. You could say I make things with my hands: I make things disappear from the hallways. I'm responsible for what you *don't* smell in the air. I carefully paint fixtures you never notice in the bathroom. This is work I'm proud of—not because it's of any consequence, but because I do it well.

We ourselves are invisible. My friends and I are the rebellious children of the working class from whom all the latest fads were stolen. In the eighties, we were the crazies who built our own indoor worm-driven compost bins and subverted the Americana we grew up with. In the nineties, we worked out how to transform used vegetable oil into fuel. In the first decade of this century we retired from adventure, returned to work, and discovered that the mainstream had caught up to our tastes. The mass-produced compost units, biodiesel stations, hybrid cars, and handmade ephemera available online all provoke our nostalgia.

Most work today isn't important to *anyone*. Not to bosses, not to employees, not to clients. Even though I'm at work eight hours a day, five days a week, I spend most of my time reading books in empty classrooms, ordering heirloom vegetable seeds from my janitor's closet, dozing off in a hidden study room. No one seems to care that my shift is eight hours long and only takes me three hours to complete.

There are material benefits to this kind of job, too. For example, none of my friends will ever pay for toilet paper or cleaning supplies again. An office chair with a small tear goes to a neighbor. When new sofas arrive, it's Christmas all over again with the old ones. It's not the spoils of the job I appreciate, but the underground gift economy they support. It's not a political issue for me so much as a way of life.

That's precisely the trouble, though. Everything in our lives is determined by work. Not just the paychecks, but also the social connections, the goods we swipe, the skills we spend our lives perfecting. Those are the things that get us from one generation to the next, but they aren't enough. They aren't enough to get us *out*.

On the other hand, I can't *not* work. I need the money. More than that, I need to fall asleep every night worn out, with a feeling of achievement. Believe it or not, maintaining a building takes a lot of skill; it can be both challenging and fulfilling. But in the three hundred or so seconds before my alarm clock sounds, I find myself wondering where else I could employ my expertise, how else I could experience a sense of accomplishment. What could I achieve besides keeping the bills paid and the students oblivious?

Every morning, the newscaster comes on before I have any answers. What is it now, this alarm clock that used to be a master, then a life coach? I'm not sure exactly. Maybe it's distracting me from figuring things out. Maybe it will ring just before I have a great idea every weekday for the rest of my life.

Every time it does, I get up and head to work. I lower my head and dunk my mop. I'm here scrubbing a floor in a university somewhere, a potential accomplice in your great getaway. A dormant comrade at the ready. A sleeper cell. But this is a challenge to you, too—to see which of us can answer these questions first, who can show how to make honest work out of changing the world.

Identity

"People from Africa were not enslaved because they were black;
they were defined as black because they were enslaved."
                                        -Noel Ignatiev

Transcending the categories of identity is no simple task.
They may be constructs, but in a manner of speaking they're
more real than reality. Race, for example, is a biological
fiction but a social fact. Some of our notions of identity
have developed over hundreds or thousands of years, to
the point that we can't imagine the world without them. It
can be hard to remember that these are not "natural," not
inescapable facts of life.

The forms of identity we know are founded on the division
between self and other, in-group and out-group—such as the
distinction between Christians and "heathens" that served to
justify conquering and butchering the latter. Blackness was
invented as a rationale for the subjugation of certain peoples,
and whiteness as an alliance among various ethnicities
on the basis of shared privilege—as illustrated by the way
additional ethnicities were subsequently inducted into this
alliance. White indentured servants hardly benefited from
this privilege the way white landowners did, but they were
systematically segregated from black slaves and granted
just enough advantages over the latter to ensure that the
white and black exploited wouldn't rise up together. These

categories later served to divide sharecroppers and factory workers the same way.

For a long time, identity within capitalism was determined largely in relation to production. Peasants, merchants, and nobles were identified as such by what they made or owned; blue-collar, white-collar, and pink-collar workers still are. When people are categorized by their roles in production, identifying yourself according to other criteria can be a form of rebellion: hence the religious dissidents of the 15th century and the hippies of the mid-20th. But recently, consumption has become more central to the construction of identity—"I drive a truck during the day, but I'm a country music fan all the time." While roles in production have become less fixed and reliable, other ways of identifying have been incorporated into capitalism: today we are encouraged to mix and match an almost infinite range of consumer identities, and these show up as personalized advertisements on our Facebook pages.

In the 21st century, longstanding categories of identity correlate less with roles in production, yet the essential imbalances of capitalism remain. Slavery has been abolished and a black man can become president, but more black men are in prison than ever before. Women can vote, work outside the home, and even become Prime Minister, so long as they advance the same agenda as male politicians.

From national liberation movements to the Black Panthers and the Lesbian Avengers, identity has been a rallying point for collective struggle. But those who only oppose capitalism because it hinders people like themselves from becoming capitalists are easy to co-opt. Kill or imprison the Panthers, permit a few Bill Cosbys and Michael Jordans to rise to the top, and the rest of the community will get the message that the only way out of poverty is through market competition. Capitalism foments divisions between people to facilitate the concentration of wealth, but it can also permit individuals economic mobility in ways that protect its intrinsic inequalities.

Once the radical wing of an identity-based movement has been isolated and defeated, the power structure can absorb the reformist remainder. In pushing for better opportunities inside a capitalist framework, reformists serve to validate capitalism, defending the benefits *some* may accrue as gains for *all* of a given identity. At worst, the discourse of privilege can be hijacked to delegitimize genuine resistance: how dare white people attack multiracial police in retaliation for their murdering a black man? Ironically, this kind of identity politics has even made its way back into discussions of class. Some activists focus on "classism" rather than capitalism, as if the poor were simply a social group and *bias* against them a bigger problem than the structures that produce poverty.

Although they are all most of us have to define ourselves, the identities produced by capitalism tend to reproduce it. If we want to get beyond it, the point is not just to fight for our interests as workers, or women, or immigrants; these can all be realized within its framework as better wages, higher glass ceilings, and citizenship. Capitalists may grant concessions, but they'll attempt to impose the costs of these on others among the exploited: for example, in response to student protests against university cutbacks in California, politicians proposed to privatize the state prisons in order to shift money into the education budget. We have to supersede our current roles and identities, reinventing ourselves and our interests through the process of resistance. We shouldn't base our solidarity on shared attributes or social positions, but on a shared refusal of our roles in the economy.

An ineffective way to deal with your privilege

Vertical Alliances, Horizontal Conflicts

On every fault line of oppression, some of the oppressed are bought off with special privileges in return for submission. The oppressed oppress their fellows, the oppressors are always oppressed by someone else; this is the nature of hierarchy. In the poorest nations, an accomplice class cashes in by selling their countrymen cheap; in the poorest neighborhoods, there are police informants; in the poorest households, men perpetuate the cross-class alliance of patriarchy.

Meanwhile, conflict between those on an equal economic footing takes a thousand forms: competition for jobs and promotions, gang warfare, ethnic strife, wars between poor nations for the resources not pillaged by more powerful ones. This discord distracts attention from the violence inherent in exploitation. It can give the impression that human beings are naturally violent and quarrelsome—certainly too much so to unite against their exploiters, let alone establish a cooperative rather than competitive way of life. Yet economic inequalities are behind most of these hostilities, however much they seem a byproduct of "human nature."

Vertical alliances and horizontal conflicts aren't just advantageous to capitalism; they're its very essence. This system only functions because people compete against others like themselves while respecting the privileges of those who have more power. Capitalism succeeded the previous systems for maintaining imbalances because it's more effective at promoting horizontal struggle and vertical obedience. In a society characterized by inequalities, the more mobility a person has the less incentive she has to find common cause with her peers—and the more incentive she has to compete against them.

Vertical alliances can take seemingly innocuous forms such as sports team followings and religious denominations. Who doesn't wish for peace on earth and goodwill towards men? Yet these forms of togetherness smooth over the disparities that prevent the song from coming true. Likewise, cultural narratives such as the promotion of "family values" forge cross-class alliances between socially conservative poor people and wealthy politicians all too eager to focus anger elsewhere. Even alliances based on oppositional or marginalized identities can serve to suppress class conflict, as demonstrated by the assimilationist wing of the gay rights movement.

When the exploited and excluded do not engage the wealthy in class warfare, they often go after each other. The history of witch hunts, pogroms, racism, sexism, and ethnic cleansing cannot be separated from the history of capitalism. These have often been driven by exactly the same economic pressures and frustrations that would otherwise produce revolutionary movements: the evils of money-lending are projected onto Jews, just as Korean businesses in black neighborhoods are held accountable for all the injustices of capitalism. In *Patriarchy and Accumulation on a World Scale*, Maria Mies quotes a German official, Bailiff Geiss, urging his lord to initiate witch hunts:

> *If only your lordship would be willing to start the burning, we would gladly provide the firewood and bear all other costs, and your lordships would earn so much that the bridge and also the Church could be well repaired. Moreover, you would get so much that you could pay*

your servants a better salary in the future, because one could confiscate whole houses and particularly the well-to-do ones.

Tragically, it's safer for lackeys to coax their masters to rob other poor people in hopes that some of the spoils will trickle down than it is for them to turn on their masters. This may be the essential paradox blocking the way to anticapitalist resistance. If what you want is more wealth, it's easier to wrest it from those worse off than yourself than to take on the ones who own most of it. But if you don't want to reproduce capitalist behavior on a smaller scale, you have to go after the ones above you, David against Goliath.

Easier than turning on your oppressors

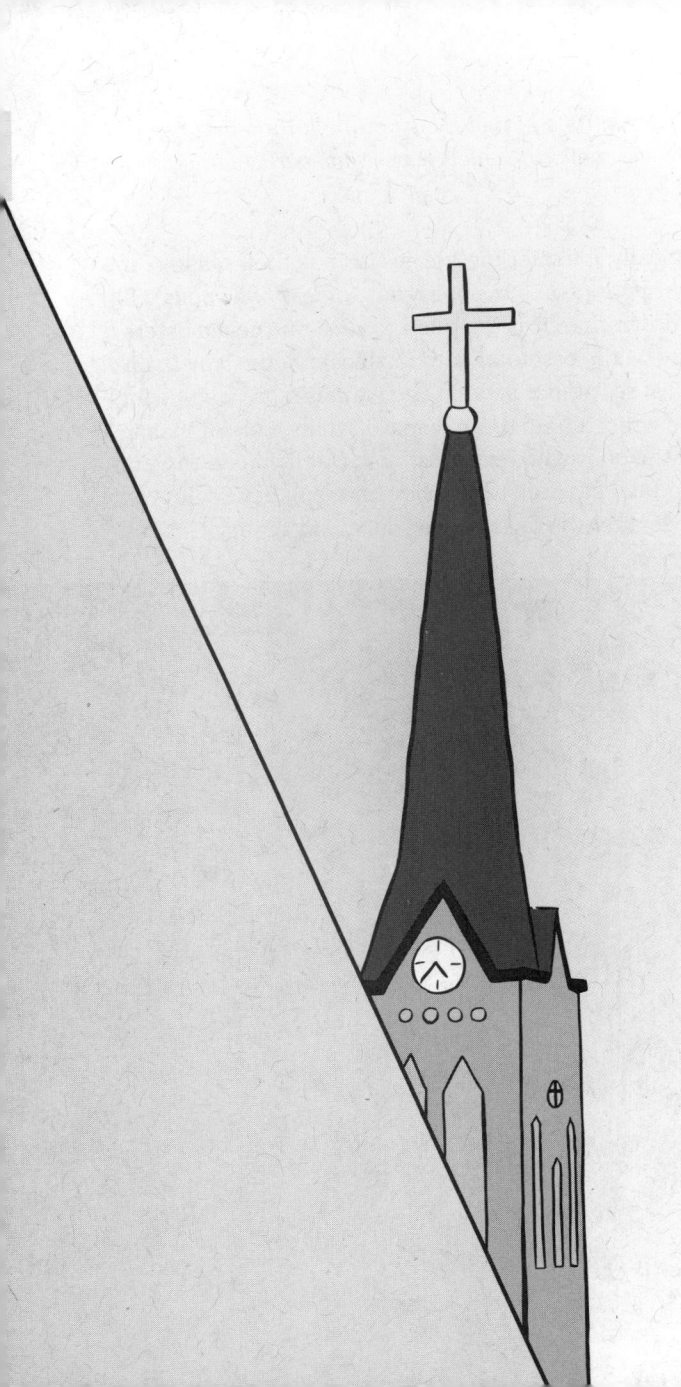

Religion

The true faith of a society, the value system upon which it is premised, becomes invisible by virtue of its ubiquity. In Europe, Christianity used to be that foundation, and even the most extreme resistance movements framed their projects in religious terms. In that sense, you could argue that capitalism is the real religion of our era: all sorts of doctrines and traditions compete, but everyone takes for granted what happens at the checkout counter, and even the imaginations of the most radical dissidents stop short of a world without work.

The Catholic Church served as the ideological foundation of feudalism; at that time, it was the biggest landowner and longest-running hierarchical organization in Europe. The clergy brought in tremendous revenues via tithes and charging for sacraments. The concentration of power was maintained by what you might call a spiritual economy, with the sacred as the determinant currency; the flow of material resources into the hands of popes and priests was a result of their monopoly on *salvation*.

Now things are reversed and it is chiefly financial power that determines the distribution of other currencies. Nothing is more sacred than property, nothing more universally valued and defended. Churches have to compete against each other on the market, sometimes as transparently for-profit ventures—as exemplified by Pat Robertson and Oral Roberts, who updated evangelism for the era of mass media. Despite the efforts of televangelists, permissive consumerism has largely replaced religious Puritanism; enjoyment of almost any kind is permitted, provided it takes place inside the framework of the market.

You can't just argue against a foundational myth; to unmask it as superstition, you have to defy it. Yet today as in the Medieval age, if anyone really threatens the sanctity of the ruling order, the authorities will call in the army. The 16th and 20th centuries both saw massive revolts and bloodbaths as the oppressed rose up first against the clergy and later against the capitalist class. All that has really changed is the value system by which brute force legitimizes itself, duping its subjects into internalizing its rule.

The only religions that have survived in the West are the ones willing to make themselves accomplices of this force, whether by taking the lead in conquest and colonization or by preaching some form of withdrawal and nonresistance. In the US, networks of politically mobilized churches still form the social base of the right wing. The European notion of the sacred is inextricably tied to domination and submission; the word "hierarchy" is derived from the roots *sacred* and *ruler*. Of course, subtle forms of dissent persist even in the most oppressive contexts, and there are believers who use the word "God" where others say mutual aid and community. But the ways churches incarnate these values—for example, by setting up assistance programs to pick up the slack left by the dismantled welfare system—generally steer people away from standing up for themselves.

Elsewhere, traditional religions have come to the fore as the fiercest opposition to Western capitalist encroachment. Much of the orthodox fundamentalism in the so-called Third World is relatively new, arising in the vacuum left by failed secular liberation movements. Yet from Iran to Afghanistan, the religious groups that present themselves as the alternative to Western capitalism still favor the centralization of power, championing older hierarchies against newer ones.

Justice

"One law for them, another for us." In theory, a rich man faces the same legal consequences for stealing a loaf of bread or sleeping under a bridge as a poor man. In practice it's not nearly that fair.

This shouldn't be surprising in view of the origins of our legal system. Human beings have always had institutions for addressing conflict, but modern jurisprudence was built around the notion of private property. The original court was the royal court, where landowners brought disputes before the king; eventually judges were appointed to make decisions in his stead. In this sense, feudalism is still with us, as we inherited its legal system and concepts of ownership along with many of its laws.

Our current legal code still protects property rights above all: it's legal to evict a family from their home, but illegal to squat an empty building. But today the mechanisms of surveillance and enforcement extend deeper than ever before into the social terrain. The king could only intercede in his subjects' affairs in exceptional cases; now millions of people and machines are ceaselessly engaged in monitoring, investigating, evaluating, and punishing.

At the top of this apparatus is the court system. The courts exert a tremendous influence on society, most of which is invisible. You can go through daily life without ever running into a judge, but the decisions of judges shape the spaces you live and work in, the technologies you use, even the ingredients in the foods you eat. Courts subsidize industries by imposing the costs of their activities on the general public, releasing them from liability for damage and danger—ironically justifying this on the grounds of their "utility" to society. Courts set social policies, defining legitimacy and deviancy. We're told judges are disinterested and unbiased—but they all belong to the same class, and where they stand is clear enough.

Nowhere are class imbalances more apparent than in the criminal justice system they oversee. The apparatus that is supposed to guarantee equal rights is so Byzantine that only a specially-trained elite has any idea how it works—or any legal right to operate in it. If you have to navigate this system, your only hope is to hire one of these specialists. If you're pitted against an adversary who can afford a more powerful lawyer—such as a corporation or government—so much the worse for you. Those too poor to afford legal counsel are lucky if they can get overworked, under-equipped public defenders. Defendants who must depend on these have higher rates of conviction and sentencing, and when they're found guilty they may be charged for their defense anyway.

In effect, this means that legal leverage is available on a dollar-for-dollar basis. To establish "equality before the law" in any meaningful sense, we would have to start by doing away with private engagement of legal counsel. But it might be easier to abolish capitalism altogether than to make a reform like that when lawyers wield so much influence.

Judges and lawyers aren't the only ones who profit from the justice industry. In the unusual case that a wealthy person is arrested, he can put up some of his wealth as a guarantee and receive it back at the conclusion of the case. Poor people who can't afford bail, however, must pay bail bondsmen and never get their money back—so the wealthy break even while businessmen accumulate wealth from the poor, as usual. This policy also pressures poor defendants who can't afford to pay bail bondsmen to take plea deals rather than languishing in jail.

Indeed, today's criminal justice system depends on most defendants pleading guilty; it could never accommodate a trial for everyone charged with a crime. Poor defendants are bullied every step of the way in order to intimidate them into accepting plea bargains. Behind the scenes, there's little pretense that the courts are impartial. In this regard, incarceration, probation, parole, fines, and other punishments serve to distribute rights and power unevenly, the same way money does.

This explains why the justice industry does so little to curb antisocial activity: its purpose is not to assist or rehabilitate people so much as to perpetuate a certain social order. In a sense, every time a person commits a crime, the society that produced him is also guilty of it; but eradicating crime is not a priority except when it threatens capitalist power relations.

Witness, for example, all the crimes corporations and governments perpetrate even by their own measure. One need only count all the treaties with Native Americans that have been broken or scrutinize the conduct of a single police department to see how little weight the law carries with those who frame and enforce it. The law offers one means of protecting the interests of those who control capital, but they bypass it quickly enough when other means are more effective. If we're told laws exist to serve everyone equally, this is simply to persuade us of their legitimacy.

Although many give lip service to this legitimacy, few accept it unconditionally. Consider how many people download software and music without paying for it, despite corporate propaganda describing this as theft. Even the staunchest defenders of law and order break traffic laws. Say what you want about the regulations applying equally to all; in practice, everyone fancies himself the exception to the rule. This matches the spirit of laws designed to be enforced on others.

Those who defend the legitimacy of laws assert that there has to be some way to prevent behavior that is dangerous or morally wrong. But laws themselves don't stop anyone from doing anything—and a citizen who takes it upon herself to enforce a law outside the court system is likely to be punished as a vigilante. The real role of the legal system is to monopolize the legitimate use of force. When a police officer expresses outrage at the "violence" of protesters who damage military equipment, it is not really their *violence* he objects to but their *self-determination.* The legal system is intended to discourage self-determination, to accustom people to the idea that they're not entitled to decide for themselves how to act.

Living under this system, we forget what it means to be responsible for ourselves. We forget how to work out conflicts according to the needs of those involved, without recourse to armed gangs of "disinterested" outsiders—we forget that such a thing is even possible. Worst of all, we forget how to stand up for ourselves when we get a raw deal, how to do as our hearts dictate regardless of the rules.

WHAT WAS
HIS CRIME?

NOT OVERTHROWING
CAPITALISM.

Illegal Capitalism

> *"As through this world I've traveled*
> *I've seen lots of funny men*
> *Some will rob you with a six-gun*
> *And some with a fountain pen"*
> – Woody Guthrie

Illegal activity extends from the bottom of the pyramid to the very top, from gangbanging to white collar crime. Bank robbery can be read as a clumsy effort to redistribute wealth, but the mafia is a capitalist venture, pure and simple. What's illegal is not necessarily bad for capitalism; a vast part of the capitalist economy exists outside the law.

What enterprise was not originally founded on some kind of theft? If laws serve to protect the property rights of those who already hold power, this makes them little more than a barrier of entry into the propertied class—one barrier among many. And even though the legal system is predominantly determined by that class, time and again its most legitimate and respected members can't help violating their own laws. Enron and Bernie Madoff are exceptions because we know about them, not because they broke the rules.

The same economic laws govern the black market as the rest of the market, producing the same concentrations of power. Successful drug cartels are structurally identical to publicly traded companies. The primary difference is that they have to enforce their interests themselves, while legal corporations outsource that need to the state.

This can give the impression that illegal enterprises are more violent than legal ones. But this violence is always the result of turf wars, business disagreements, or crackdowns—that is to say, the underlying cause is always a business concern. In this regard, illegal capitalists are no different from their legal counterparts. If General Motors had no legal system through which to enforce patent rights, they would surely take matters into their own hands, or be supplanted by a company that would. The legal apparatus of the state

Foreword

As officers and employees of Enron Corp., its subsidiaries, and its affiliated companies, we are responsible for conducting the business affairs of the companies in accordance with all applicable laws and in a moral and honest manner.

To be sure that we understand what is expected of us, Enron has adopted certain policies, with the approval of the Board of Directors, which are set forth in this booklet. I ask that you read them carefully and completely and that, as you do, you reflect on your past actions to make certain that you have complied with the policies. It is absolutely essential that you fully comply with these policies in the future. If you have any questions, talk them over with your supervisor, manager, or Enron legal counsel.

We want to be proud of Enron and to know that it enjoys a reputation for fairness and honesty and that it is respected. Gaining such respect is one aim of our advertising and public relations activities, but no matter how effective they may be, Enron's reputation finally depends on its people, on you and me. Let's keep that reputation high.

July 1, 2000

Kenneth I. Lay

Kenneth L. Lay
Chairman and Chief
Executive Officer

2

is like a vast, monopolized version of the same structures used by the mafia. The black market isn't necessarily any more violent than the rest of the economy: what are drive-by shootings next to the prison-industrial complex? The same violence that shocks us in criminals is invisible in society at large because it is ubiquitous and constant.

Much of the law is determined by the conveniences of the capitalist class. For example, tobacco has always been legal because it's produced domestically by US corporations; coca products, grown in South America, are illegal—except for Coca-Cola. You could argue that cocaine is illegal because it's so harmful to consumers, but cigarette manufacturers are permitted to add extra chemicals to make their carcinogenic products more addictive. Petroleum is turning out to be more addictive and destructive than tobacco or coca, and there's no chance of it becoming illegal. Many capitalist products are hazardous, but nothing is more hazardous than capitalism: as William Burroughs put it, *selling is more addictive than using.*

Cultural norms are another rationale for prohibiting an industry. Often, this is simply a matter of politicians taking advantage of popular prejudices to protect a niche in the market: sex work may be illegal, but there's always a certain "massage parlor" that operates with impunity. Enforcing these prohibitions also opens up profitable opportunities, and the resulting mechanisms of repression can easily be shifted from criminals to other targets. The War on Drugs was used to terrorize poor black communities in the US and attack social movements in Latin America—at the same time that the CIA was permitting the Nicaraguan Contras to smuggle cocaine into the US in return for arms.

The law of the courts is ultimately subordinate to the laws of supply and demand. If someone discovers an effective way to make money that violates the law, the authorities eventually have to condone it—whether tacitly or openly—unless it impedes the functioning of the rest of the economy. For example, in Mexico and Russia the black market has grown to rival the rest of the market in scale. Just as US companies are more powerful than the US government, Mexican drug cartels can meet the Mexican government in open warfare. In this context, Mexican politicians have begun discussing drug legalization as a strategy to stop dividing capitalist interests.

In the logic of the market, people make decisions by balancing risk against reward. Every person and corporation has a particular tolerance for different kinds and degrees of risk; there are investment funds that deal only in investments that are unlikely to pay off, and brokers who deal only in very safe treasury bonds almost certain to earn a small profit. Participants in the black market have assessed their risk tolerances according to their circumstances and concluded that the potential yield is worth the risks involved.

But over time, risks and rewards can change as laws and norms shift; for example, when the government decriminalizes a drug, new investors bring more capital into that market. Ironically, legalizing the industries in which poor people with few legal options make a living can leave them worse off, luring in powerful competitors able to put them out of a job. Plenty of poor people have paid to raise their kids by selling marijuana on the side, but if it were fully legalized the tobacco companies would divide up the market in a matter of weeks.

Just as the black market is a part of the capitalist economy, it is a site of anticapitalist struggles. Independent petty criminals defy hierarchical mafias; sex workers collectivize to escape their pimps. In Copenhagen's famous occupied neighborhood Christiania, marijuana dealers have coexisted with squatters for decades, maintaining a sort of autonomous zone; in Dublin and elsewhere, grassroots resistance has forced heroin dealers out of neighborhoods. None of these provides a model of life outside capitalism, but they show that wherever there are inequalities, there is resistance.

US businessman:
"But isn't your society riddled with corruption? Don't you have to bribe officials at every turn?"

Chinese businessman:
"Corruption? We have the same system you have, only ours is more *democratic.* In our country, anyone can 'lobby' for his needs on an itemized basis. In yours, the system's so bureaucratic that only the incredibly wealthy can influence political affairs. But I bet lobbying accounts for at least as much of your GDP."

"For a youth with no other hope in a system that excludes them, the gang becomes their corporation, college, religion, and life... I now have 'Eight Trays' written across my neck and 'Crips' on my chest. Ever see George Bush with 'Republican' on his chest or 'Capitalist' on his neck?"
– Sanyika Shakur

Back when Christianity was still central to the workings of white supremacy, the young Harriet Tubman began experiencing visions which she attributed to the all-powerful God spoken of in the white churches. By the time of the Civil War, Tubman had escaped slavery, smuggled more than seventy people to freedom, rescued her parents from the authorities, and helped John Brown attempt to start a slave rebellion. People called her Moses after the biblical prophet who delivered the Hebrews from slavery in Egypt.

Tubman incarnated the mythology of her former captors in defiance of them, fulfilling the values they purported to hold. Today many black children grow up on the mythology of the self-made millionaire, yet find themselves with hardly any legal options for economic advancement. On the street corners of the poorest neighborhoods, urban youth employ the same competitive strategies that appear in Wall Street boardrooms. Applying the logic of capitalism outside the laws of the state is denounced and targeted not so much because it is *dangerous*—there is no safe form of capitalism—but because this practice is the only thing "legitimate" capitalists can't monopolize for themselves. A century ago, black churches were burned to the ground as white Christians came to terms with the fact that they had *become Pharaoh*. Today, black children are put in prison for becoming Henry Ford.

Theft

Not all illegal activity adheres to a capitalist model. Shoplifting, embezzlement, and workplace theft outrank charity and welfare as the primary ways wealth is redistributed down the pyramid. The tremendous numbers of people who participate in illegal file-sharing show how naturally people take to free distribution—it is, after all, the way our species circulated goods for most of its existence. Theft can be an expression of materialism, but it also implies that human needs are more important than property rights; when there are so many goods in the world and so many of them go to waste, why shouldn't people take what they want?

The majority of theft is carried out by employees targeting their own employers—each year millions of workers pilfer billions of dollars of goods and services from their workplaces. Employees know they're getting ripped off; despite the risks, most can't help snatching back a little of what they produce. The security cameras pointed at every cash register bear witness to this.

The US Chamber of Commerce estimates that 75 percent of all employees steal at least once, and that half of these steal repeatedly. Meanwhile, the richest 1% of US citizens own more financial wealth than all the bottom 95% combined. That means the wealth of the upper upper class is greater than *all* the wealth of the upper class and middle class *added* to all of the wealth of the working class and underclass.

Can you imagine how much more unequal that distribution would be if people didn't steal?

Of course, stealing hardly levels the playing field. The higher your social position, the better your opportunities are to steal and the less danger you're in if you get caught. Steal five bucks, go to jail—steal five million, go to Congress. Yet the worse off you are, the harder it is to make ends meet *without* stealing.

The universal moral proscription against theft is intended to protect the collective interests of humanity against individual thieves. Ironically, when an employee turns in a coworker for theft, that prescription ends up protecting the individual interests of a few capitalists against the collective interests of their employees, whose labor it is that produces the wealth they hoard in the first place. The wealth of a corporation is made up of profit derived from workers who are not paid the full value of their labor and consumers who pay more than the production cost of their purchases. Redistributing this is not stealing so much as it is reversing the effects of thefts already in progress. Workplace theft is thus a challenge to the morality of capitalist meritocracy; it suggests a profound discontent with capitalism.

But as long as the expressions of that discontent are isolated and secretive, they cannot interrupt the status quo. If stealing from work is what workers do instead of revolting—treating the symptoms of exploitation rather than the condition—it can even serve the bosses' interests, giving employees a pressure valve to blow off steam and enabling them to survive to work another day without a wage increase. Capitalists figure the costs of this "shrinkage" into their business plans; they know stealing is an inevitable side effect of exploitation that poses little danger of bringing it to an end.

On the other hand, the notion that stealing doesn't count as class struggle enforces a dichotomy between "legitimate" workplace organizing on one hand and concrete acts of

If you don't steal from your boss
You're stealing from your family

resistance, revenge, and survival on the other. Wherever this division exists, labor organizing tends to prioritize bureaucracy over initiative, representation over autonomy, appeasement over confrontation, legitimacy in capitalists' eyes over effectiveness.

What would it look like to approach labor organizing the way people go about stealing from their bosses? It would mean focusing on resistance tactics that meet individual needs, starting from what we can do ourselves with each other's assistance. It would mean adopting strategies that provide immediate material or emotional benefit *on our own terms*. It would mean building connections through the process of attempting to seize back the environments we work and live in, rather than within organizations that endlessly defer struggle.

A workforce that organized this way would be impossible to co-opt or dupe. No boss could threaten it with anything, for its power would derive directly from its own actions, not from compromises that gave the bosses hostages and offered prominent organizers incentives not to fight. It would be a boss's worst nightmare—and a union official's, too.

And what would it look like to go about stealing from work as if it were a way to change the world rather than simply survive in it? So long as employees solve their problems individually, they can only confront them individually. Stealing in secret keeps class struggle a private affair—the question is how to make it into a public project that gains momentum. This shifts the focus from *what* to *how*. A small item stolen with the support of one's coworkers is more significant than a huge heist carried out in secret. Stolen goods shared in a way that builds a sense of common interests are worth more than a high-dollar embezzlement that only benefits one employee the way a raise or promotion would.

Work is stealing from workers. Workers have a whole world to steal back from work.

THIS IS A TALE OF TWO CITIES. Both are nominally suburbs of the same Rust Belt metropolis, but large enough to be major cities themselves. They share the same local bus system and the same daily newspaper. What separates them is ten miles of suburban sprawl and a tremendous chasm of class privilege.

The first city, which I will call Huffmanville, is what comes to mind when you hear the word "suburb." Mansions with chemical-green lawns are dotted along mile after mile of winding lanes without sidewalks. The small central business district is promoted throughout the greater metropolitan area as a "shopping destination," and the town itself is consistently ranked by national business magazines as a desirable place to live and own property. Historic buildings, in which generations-old businesses were long ago forced out by high rents, now house high-end clothing retailers, specialty wine shops, and a Barnes & Noble bookstore. Trendy and expensive restaurants rival those of the metropolis. Attractive white people can be seen jogging on a network of recreational bike trails, spandex on their buttocks and electronics on their heads.

The other city, which I will call New Stolp, is what demographers call a "satellite city" rather than a true suburb. This means it used to be a separate city before the expanding suburbs caught up with it, and there is still a large, relatively old and dense urban core. For those of you on the East Coast, think Newark or Paterson; if you're on the West Coast, think San Bernardino.

This urban part of New Stolp is mainly lower- and working-class, and includes a large Mexican immigrant population. The billboards in town are in Spanish, and the main drag is lined with carnicerías, liquor stores, pawn shops, and predatory "payday loan" vendors. The Latin Kings are active there, and high-school students at New Stolp East are subjected to searches using metal detectors upon arrival each morning. Police prowl neighborhoods to keep an eye on the residents rather than possible intruders, and routinely flush sleeping vagrants from the bus station and the parks. In the downtown area, the old stone and masonry buildings are mostly vacant. Business leaders have been clamoring about "revitalization" for years, and the process of gentrification has only recently begun along the river's edge.

The people in the suburban sprawl outside New Stolp don't identify with the urban core. They always make some kind of qualifying statement when they tell you where they live: "It's not *New Stolp* New Stolp; it's actually a nice area…" Finally, as if to formalize this division, a county line runs through the municipal area so that Huffmanville and the suburban part of New Stolp are in one county and the old, poor, urban part of New Stolp is in another.

A few years ago, I was a commuter across this gap between worlds: I lived and worked in the urban part of New Stolp and attended a private liberal-arts college with a leafy campus in Huffmanville. Tuition there was expensive, and it wasn't the kind of place that gave out a lot of scholarships or financial aid money. But I was determined not to go into debt to pay for it—I already knew that debt makes you a slave. I decided before I even enrolled that I wasn't going to take out any loans, ever: I would only continue going to school if I could pay for it at the bursar's office in cash.

So for a long time I only took one three-credit course per semester; that was all I could afford. I rode the bus into Huffmanville on the days I had class, and worked all the days

I didn't. It was demoralizing. Things could have gone on that way—one course a semester, three days a week—and in ten years or so I might eventually have graduated. But this was unacceptable to me. *Why should that pretty, leafy campus be accessible only to the children of rich Huffmanville parents?* I fumed, realizing that if I wanted to graduate any time soon I was going to have to do something else. I needed to find another way to feed the swine at the bursar's office. I would have to *make my own financial aid.*

Within a year of that decision I successfully embezzled over twenty-five thousand dollars from my place of employment, a hardware store owned by two Huffmanville businessmen at which I worked as a cashier. I was never caught or fired. I graduated from college a year later.

&

The store where I worked was part of a regional chain of about a dozen others, all based around a flagship store in Huffmanville. Definitely not a mom-and-pop operation, but not Wal-Mart, either. In fact, looking back, the size of the company was probably ideal: if it had been much smaller (a single store, or even a handful), I might have felt guilty about stealing from them—making things even tougher for the little guy than they already are. On the other hand, if it had been a big multinational corporation, there probably would have been too many security measures in place for me to pull it off.

As it was, the chain was wholly owned by a father-and-son team, both big shots in the local Huffmanville business elite—there was even a building at my college named after them. The father had started the chain with the main store in Huffmanville and the son was now president. This was also something that suited me: unlike many cases of workplace theft, I knew exactly who I was stealing from—I had *looked them both in the eye* when they had dropped by our store for a surprise inspection.

Likewise, the particular store I worked in was probably the one in the entire chain best suited to large-scale cash liberation. Although the chain included several stores in Huffmanville and throughout other towns and suburbs, ours was the only one in New Stolp, on the edge of one of the city's poorest neighborhoods. It received the least attention from the owners, since it made the least money—though enough for $25,000 to disappear unnoticed. The store had no security cameras; the management claimed there were hidden ones, but every employee knew this was a lie. Thanks to an old-fashioned layout and shelving nearly up to the ceiling, there were very few clear lines of sight. Finally, the cash registers used an antiquated computer system that the owners were too cheap to replace.

The standard wage for grunts like me was seven dollars per hour—just enough over the minimum wage, the managers must have thought, to buy our loyalty. When I started working there, they had me doing everything in the store. This ranged from cleaning the bathrooms and stocking merchandise to filling propane tanks for grills and cutting keys—we used a manual grinder, not the fully automated ones you see nowadays at Home Depot.

But when the managers saw how proficient I was at running the cash register and handling minor problems that arose there, they made me a permanent cashier. As they gained confidence in me, they began to give me a considerable degree of autonomy in doing my job. Eventually I was basically running the front end of the store for them single-handedly when I was on the clock. This made me a valuable employee. They liked the fact that I didn't *need* supervision, and I was just as happy not to have it. I taught myself how to troubleshoot the computer system; I made snap judgments and took care of problems with customers on my own without having to radio the manager on duty for help.

Fortunately, they never considered that this problem-solving ability of mine could be put to other uses.

※

I am what you'd call good with numbers: remembering them, adding and subtracting them, keeping accurate running totals. I can do all this in my head—a skill which would prove useful, given that my job involved handling a nearly ceaseless flow of cash with minimal supervision. In some ways, this is one of the oldest stories in capitalism: the savvy accountant ripping off his less-mathematically-inclined wealthy clients. But there were also important differences. By this time I'd had a while to develop my political views; I considered my interests to be fundamentally opposed to those of the store owners. I wanted to inflict as many losses on them as I could possibly get away with, even in ways that didn't directly benefit me.

One of the ways I did this was by charging customers less for their purchases than I was supposed to. Like I said, I was very good at my job—and as anyone who has ever worked as a cashier knows, all this really means is that I was good at getting customers through the line *quickly*. Sometimes my hands moved items over the counter and into bags so fast that half of them didn't scan, and the customer got a little unexpected discount. Other times an item wouldn't scan, so I'd either make up a low price for it or—if the customer struck me as sensible and no one else was watching—just drop it into a bag and shrug. Is that belt sander coming up in the computer as invalid? Just ring it up as $2.00 under "miscellaneous" and you're good to go!

Some items in the store—such as nuts and bolts—didn't have bar codes, so we used the "honor system," relying on customers to write the correct prices on the bag. This was ridiculous, not least because the sign telling them to do so was only in English while most of our customers spoke Spanish as their first language. If customers wrote down the prices I had to charge what they wrote, but when they didn't I was free to charge whatever I wanted. Say a person had what looked like forty screws worth 59 cents each in a bag; I'd ring up twenty "miscellaneous hardware" items at five cents each. Most customers were all too happy to accept the new prices I offered them. A few were confused, however, and stood examining the receipt after I had handed them their change, wondering why they hadn't been charged more. *Don't question it,* I tried to convey with a quick look of the eyes. *Just take your shit and go.*

It was always important for me to maintain the *appearance* of doing my job accurately and correctly. For instance, I'd always be very careful if there were other people in line—let's face it, some customers are as good as snitches. This may sound bad, but I was always warier to give unauthorized discounts to customers if they were white—I guessed that white people would be the most likely to inform on me. Why certain people feel they have to protect the interests of store owners at the expense of themselves, the employees, and everyone else is beyond me, but some do.

My fellow employees soon figured out that I'd turn a blind eye to almost anything that could be carried out the front door and into their cars. Likewise, when I noticed customers who looked like they were trying to shoplift, I would step away from the register and pretend to be busy doing something else so they could "sneak past" without my noticing. I stole whatever I needed, too—paint, tools, light bulbs, and so on—but I didn't sell them or anything like that. To get the money, I had to use other tactics.

In the primitive computer program that the cash registers used, it took only a single keystroke at any time during a sale to turn that sale into a refund of the same amount. In mathematical terms, all of the signs on the prices would be flipped instantaneously from positive to negative, meaning that the computer expected money to be removed from the drawer rather than put in. So, naturally, if the cashier wanted the amount of cash in the drawer to stay the same as the amount on the sales summary at the end of the day, he or she would just have to take the amount in question out of the drawer and stick it in a pocket.

A simple concept, but surprisingly difficult to execute repeatedly without getting caught. How did I manage to pilfer twenty-five grand this way? The answer lies in the principle of sustainability: being patient, knowing when enough is enough, being aware of your limits and not exceeding them. Other cashiers stole money this way too—obviously, I wasn't the first person to think of it—but they were too greedy, or too obvious, or too impatient. Some emptied half their drawers in a shift and got busted. I was able to skim over a hundred dollars a day off the top while maintaining the outward appearance of a diligent worker and arousing no suspicion.

During this period, the store was robbed. The robbers were smart: they hit the store at closing time on the biggest shopping day of the Christmas season, when the safe was as chock-full of cash as it would ever be. I wasn't there that night, and the owners didn't disclose how much was taken, but from my knowledge of the store's operations it couldn't have been more than five or six thousand dollars. It still brings a smile to my face to know that I got away with far more loot than those robbers ever did. True, it took longer—but I didn't have to scare anyone or run the risk of somebody getting killed.

I truly felt bad for the assistant manager who had a gun stuck in her face; she didn't deserve it. To my knowledge she never received any acknowledgement from the owners that she had had her life threatened because of *their* money. She even had to open the next day.

As far as I know, none of the managers at the store ever discovered what I was up to. If they did, they had no way of proving it—I was too careful—but my guess is that they had no clue. Anyone familiar with hourly-wage workplace dynamics knows that even the weakest circumstantial evidence is sufficient for a boss to terminate an employee. If they had suspected anything, they'd have done *something* about it. Realistically, they probably assumed I engaged in some minor theft—try finding an employee who doesn't, especially in a place like New Stolp—but they clearly had no inkling of the *scale*, or else I would have been given the boot and possibly faced criminal charges.

Perhaps it's ironic that when I stopped working at the store it was because I had achieved my goal: I was finally a full-time student in my senior year, thanks to the money I'd stolen. But the *really* ironic part is that I now regret what I did—not stealing money, but spending it on college tuition. I dream about all the *other* things I could have done with twenty-five thousand dollars besides handing it over for a degree I now consider next to worthless. I could have bought a house and started a collective; I could have opened a coffee shop with a reading library; I could have given the money to a struggling free clinic or community center. I should have done something with it to connect with other people like me rather than trying to get ahead by myself.

Today I'm still on the job market. People in New Stolp are still doing landscaping and housecleaning for people in Huffmanville. I may have pulled one over on my employer, but the bursar's office got the last laugh.

Gentrification

It sounds so innocuous, so beneficial: "revitalization." Who wouldn't want their neighborhood to have better stores and public facilities, less crime, higher property values?

Renters, that's who—and low-income homeowners who can't afford higher property taxes, and anyone the police will target when they step up patrols to protect the new arrivals. As wealthy people buy up real estate in poor neighborhoods, the cost of living is driven up and the previous inhabitants are driven out. Revitalization doesn't mean that the residents get to enjoy a better standard of living, but that they have to make way for those who can afford to. Local governments often pave the way for this because it's good for business, which they call "the community."

After the Second World War, white families fled from the newly integrated inner cities to the suburbs, taking their tax dollars with them. Thanks to the proliferation of automobiles and highways, they no longer needed to live as close to workplaces and shopping centers. Those highways were often routed directly through predominantly black and Latino neighborhoods, as part of a program of destructive "neglect."

We know the rest of the story. A generation later, after poverty, gang warfare, and police incursions have decimated the original communities and cut property values, a new population of downwardly-mobile renters is pushed into the neighborhood by economic pressures. Some of these

are artists, dropouts, people trying to find a place outside the reach of capitalism—just like the refugees from Europe who helped colonize the "New World." They're followed by a wave of investors buying and renovating properties in order to speculate in the real estate market, and entrepreneurs opening businesses to cater to the new population. The free "cultural production" of the artists creates a lucrative ambience for the entrepreneurs, which will be unnecessary by the time the artists are being pushed out of the neighborhood in turn.

Gentrification mirrors the restructuring that colonization and globalization have imposed on the whole planet. Capitalists drain resources from an area, seal it off, then reappear when values have dropped enough that a small investment can easily turn a profit. Following the exodus of manufacturing jobs from North American cities, many local economies are centered around service sector industries that cater to the wealthy and privileged. These economies no longer need large concentrations of workers in long-term communities; if anything, they run more smoothly when communities are frequently uprooted and reconfigured.

At first, it would seem that if some neighborhoods are gentrifying, others must be getting cheaper—where would all those poor people go, otherwise? In some rural areas and rust belt cities, property values are indeed declining along with population; yet in most highly populated areas, the cost of living is only increasing. Gentrification is the process of the rich getting richer and the poor getting poorer embodied in real estate, as workers pay proportionately more and more of their income for space to live.

Paradoxically, the only way to protect your neighborhood from gentrification is to wreck it. You have to make it a place no one wealthier than yourself—no one who had any other option—would ever choose to live. If you put in a lot of work to improve a space you're renting or a neighborhood you'll be forced out of, you're just fattening the pockets of your exploiters. When you make a few hundred dollars unexpectedly, it's middle-class thinking to spend it on renovations—the proletarian thing to do is blow your security deposit on trashing your place, so you can be sure your landlord won't be able to rent it to wealthier people after you. That's security for the underclass!

This also explains the seemingly senseless violence in poor neighborhoods. And yet this attitude isn't likely to go over well with other poor people trying to make the best of their situation.

Gentrification contributes to complicated racial tensions; indeed, it's produced in part by the asymmetrical dynamics between race and class, as poor white people pave the way for middle-class white people in formerly non-white neighborhoods. Fighting gentrification is equally complicated. Do we blame the wave of poor people seeking affordable housing, or the speculators who follow in their wake? What if we can't distinguish between the two? Can we combat gentrification simply by pitting moral imperatives against economic pressures? Or is it unrealistic to think we could put a stop to it without abolishing capitalism itself?

Boundaries and Travel

Speak of freedom all you like—we live in a world of walls.

There used to be few enough that we could keep up with them—Hadrian's Wall, the Great Wall of China, the Berlin Wall. Now they're everywhere. The walls of the old days have not been torn down but rather "gone viral," penetrating every level of society. Wall Street, named after a stockade built by African slaves to protect European colonists, exemplifies this transformation: it's no longer a question of fences keeping out the natives, but of trade maintaining ubiquitous divisions in a society that no longer has an "outside."

These divisions take many forms. There are physical boundaries: gated communities, private malls and campuses, security checkpoints, refugee camps, borders of concrete and barbed wire. There are social boundaries: old-boy networks, neighborhoods segregated by class and race, invisible zones on the schoolyard identifying cool and uncool. There are boundaries controlling the flow of information: internet firewalls, security clearances, classified databases. From the standpoint of our rulers, the more boundaries can be imposed by unequal access to information or buying power, the better—that's more convenient than minefields and armed guards, though the latter are hardly obsolete.

Borders don't just divide countries: they exist wherever people live in fear of immigration raids, wherever people must accept lower wages because they have no documents.

Borders extend in the other direction, too: there are detention centers in northern Africa to which European nations outsource the task of controlling migrants. One has only to visit Kinshasa's slums and Oslo's Frogner Park in succession to get a sense of how many barriers there must be between them.

Of course, there are immigrants in Oslo who aren't much better off than they were at home, while an *accomplice class* in Kinshasa wields more wealth and power than the average Norwegian. The world isn't just horizontally divided into spatial zones, but socially divided into zones of privilege, of *access*. The US-Mexico border is part of the same structure as the chain-link fence that keeps a homeless person out of a parking lot and the price bracket that keeps day laborers from buying the "organic" option at the grocery store. All of these are walls.

And what's the corollary of walls? Prisoners. If a prisoner is a person contained by walls, what does that make us?

The new walls don't act on everyone the same way. Some people labor in sweatshops, fabricating products that travel further than they'll ever be permitted to; others dash around the planet, racking up frequent flier miles and jet lag. Paradoxically, the proliferation of walls seems to be accompanied by a shift towards constant movement. This affects both the poor, who have to chase jobs, and the wealthy whose job it is to chase after the market itself. In this context, the role of walls is not to block movement so much as to channel it.

Much of this travel appears voluntary; it even retains some of the romantic associations of setting out on a journey into the unknown. But considered as a whole, it looks more like the winds of the economy sweeping us willy-nilly around the world. Industrialization inflicted an earlier wave of transience, uprooting laborers from the countryside and breaking up extended families, leaving the nuclear family as the basic social unit. Today's new wave of transience is even breaking up nuclear families.

Perpetual travel and relocation fracture longstanding communities, social ties, and cultures that value activities other than exchange. A thousand miles from home, you can only eat in a restaurant, even if you'd rather pick food from a garden and cook it with friends. When everyone is constantly moving, it makes more sense to try to build up capital than to develop long-term relationships and commitments. Capital is universally exchangeable, while personal relationships are unique and non-transferable. And the more atomized we become, the more we feel compelled to uproot ourselves yet again to look elsewhere for everything we've lost.

Pollution

If people took the scientific reports about global warming seriously, the engines of every fire department would sound their sirens and race to the nearest factory to extinguish its furnaces. Every high school student would run to the thermostat, turn it off, and tear it from the classroom wall, then hit the parking lot to slash tires. Every responsible suburban parent would don safety gloves and walk around the block pulling the electrical meters out of the utility boxes behind houses and condominiums. Every gas station attendant would press the emergency button to shut off the pumps, cut the hoses, and glue the locks on the doors; every coal and petroleum corporation would immediately set about burying their unused product where it came from—using only the muscles of their own arms, of course.

But those who learn about global warming from the news are too disconnected to react. The destruction of the natural world has been going on for centuries now; you have to be alienated indeed to drive past felled trees, spewing smokestacks, and acres of asphalt every day without noticing anything until it shows up in a headline. People who draw conclusions from news articles rather than the world they see and hear and smell are bound to destroy everything they touch. That alienation is the root of the problem; the devastation of the environment simply follows from it.

When profit margins are more real than living things, when weather patterns are more real than refugees fleeing hurricanes, when emissions cap agreements are more real than new developments going up down the street, the world has already been signed over for destruction. The climate crisis isn't an event that *might* happen, looming into view ahead; it is the familiar setting of our daily lives. Deforestation isn't just taking place in national forests or foreign jungles; it is as real at every strip mall in Ohio as it is in the heart of the Amazon. The buffalo used to roam *right here.* Our detachment from the land is catastrophic whether or not the sea level is rising, whether or not the desertification and famine sweeping other continents have reached us yet.

This detachment didn't come out of nowhere; it's a corollary of the separation imposed between production and consumption. When we can only see the world through an economic lens, it becomes abstract, expendable. Some environmentalists would reduce the causes of global warming to "too much" technological development, but the problem is that capitalism imposes relationships that promote *a certain kind* of technological development. In the US, the major oil producers bought up the patents for fuel-efficient automobile engines and buried them, while automobile and oil companies successfully lobbied against public transportation. Los Angeles once had a decent public transit system, but it was dismantled under pressure from the auto industry, making way for the commuter nightmare that exists today.

As usual, the class that brought about the crisis would have us believe that they're the best qualified to remedy it. But there's no reason to believe that their motives or methods have changed. Everyone knows smoking causes cancer, but they're still selling low-tar cigarettes.

Pollution and environmental destruction are yet another case of capitalists passing costs down the pyramid to the poor. Garbage dumps are never built in wealthy neighborhoods;

neither are oil wells. Mines collapse on miners and laborers die of exposure to poisonous chemicals—and employers have the audacity to argue that environmental protections are bad for workers because they endanger their *jobs!* If it weren't for economic pressures, no one would take such jobs in the first place, nor wreak such havoc on the environment. And the workers who must take them are treated no better than the ecosystems they're paid to destroy; mountaintop removal and other destructive practices have enabled corporations to eliminate tens of thousands of jobs.

Capitalism is not sustainable. It demands constant expansion; it can reward nothing else. Beware of supposed environmentalists whose first priority is to sustain the economy. Nuclear power, solar power, "clean" coal, and wind turbines are not going to usher in a pollution-free utopia. Neither are carbon trading, biofuels, recycling programs, or organic superfoods. So long as our society is driven by the logic of profit and competition, these are all just bids to maintain the present state of affairs. But it can't go on forever.

Solutions to Global Warming!

From the makers of global warming—
"sustainable" energy!

THE **CORPORATE** SOLUTION

Where others see hardship and tragedy, entrepreneurs see opportunity. Putting the "green" in greenhouse gases and the "eco" in economy, they greet the apocalypse with outstretched wallets. Are natural disasters wrecking communities? Offer disaster relief—at a price—and put up luxury condominiums where the survivors used to live. Are food supplies contaminated with toxins? Slap "organic" on some of them and jack up the price—presto, what was once taken for granted in every vegetable is suddenly a selling point! Is consumerism devouring the planet? Time for a line of environmentally friendly products, cashing in on guilt and good intentions to move more units.

So long as being "sustainable" is a privilege reserved for the rich, the crisis can only intensify. All the better for those banking on it.

The **Conservative** Solution

Many conservatives deny that our society is causing global warming; some still don't believe in evolution, either. But what they themselves believe is immaterial; they're more concerned about what it is profitable for *others* to believe. For example, when the UN's Intergovernmental Panel on Climate Change released its 2007 report, an ExxonMobil-funded think tank linked to the Bush administration offered $10,000+ to any scientist who would dispute its findings.

That is to say—some people consider it a better investment to bribe experts to deny that anything is happening than to take any steps to avert catastrophe. Better that the apocalypse snatches us unawares so long as they can maintain their profits one more year. Sooner the end of life on earth than the possibility of life beyond capitalism!

The **Liberal** Solution

Certain do-gooders would like to claim credit for bringing global warming to the attention of the public, even though environmentalists had been clamoring about it for decades. But politicians like Al Gore aren't trying to save the environment so much as to rescue the *causes* of its destruction. They press for government and corporate recognition of the crisis because ecological collapse could destabilize capitalism if it catches them off guard. Small wonder corporate initiatives and incentives figure so prominently in the solutions they propose.

Like their conservative colleagues, liberals would sooner risk extinction than consider abandoning industrial capitalism. They're simply too invested in it to do otherwise—witness the Gore family's long-running relationship with Occidental Petroleum. In this light, their bid to seize the reins of the environmentalist movement looks suspiciously like a calculated effort to prevent a more *realistic* response to the crisis.

The **Malthusian** Solution

Some people attribute the environmental crisis to overpopulation—but how many shantytown dwellers and subsistence farmers do you have to add up to equal the ecological impact of a single high-powered executive? If there is such a thing as overpopulation at all, it's made possible by unsustainable industrial agriculture—so the Malthusians have it backwards.

The **Socialist** Solution

For centuries, socialists have promised to grant everyone access to middle-class standards of living. Now that it turns out that the biosphere can't support even a small minority pursuing that lifestyle, you'd expect socialists to adjust their notion of utopia accordingly. Instead they've simply updated it to match the latest bourgeois fashions: today every worker deserves to work a "green" job and eat organic produce.

But "green job" is an oxymoron: *working* isn't sustainable. The problem is that both private corporations and government-sponsored agencies look at the world as something to be *managed*, something from which value can be *extracted*. Likewise, "green" products only came to be as a marketing ploy to differentiate high-end merchandise from proletarian standard fare. If you're going to think big enough to imagine a society without class differences, you might as well aim for a future in which we share the wealth of a vibrant natural world rather than chopping it up into inert commodities.

The **Communist** Solution

Marxism, Leninism, and Maoism served as a convenient means to jerk "underdeveloped" nations into the industrial age, utilizing state intervention to "modernize" peoples who still retained a connection to the land before eventually dropping them unceremoniously at the margin of the free market. As the old Eastern European joke goes, socialism is the painful transition between capitalism and capitalism. Even today, despite the legacy of Chernobyl, party communists have gotten no further than blithe assurances that new management would take care of everything. Sing along to the tune of "Solidarity Forever":

> If the workers owned the factories, climate change
> would not exist
> All the smoke from all the smokestacks would be
> changed to harmless mist . . .

THE INDIVIDUAL SOLUTION

An individual can live a completely "sustainable" lifestyle without doing anything to hinder the corporations and governments responsible for the vast majority of environmental devastation. The same goes for whole communities. Keeping your hands clean—"setting an example" no statesman or tycoon will emulate—is meaningless while others lay the planet to waste. To set a better example, *stop them.*

THE RADICAL SOLUTION

Many people respond to the crisis with despair or even a kind of wrongheaded anticipation, imagining that it will bring about social change if nothing else can. Yet there's no reason to believe the exhaustion of the planet's petroleum supply will put an end to capitalism—there were economic imbalances before fossil fuels were the backbone of the economy. Likewise, it's all too plausible that these imbalances will make it through ecological collapse intact, so long as there are people left to dominate and obey.

We'll get out of the apocalypse what we put into it: we can't expect it to produce a more liberated society unless we put the foundations in place now. Forget about individualistic survival schemes that cast you as the Last Person on Earth—Hurricane Katrina showed that when the storm hits, the most important thing is to be part of a community that can defend itself. The coming upheavals may indeed offer a chance for social change, but only if we start implementing it *right now*.

Another end of the world is possible!

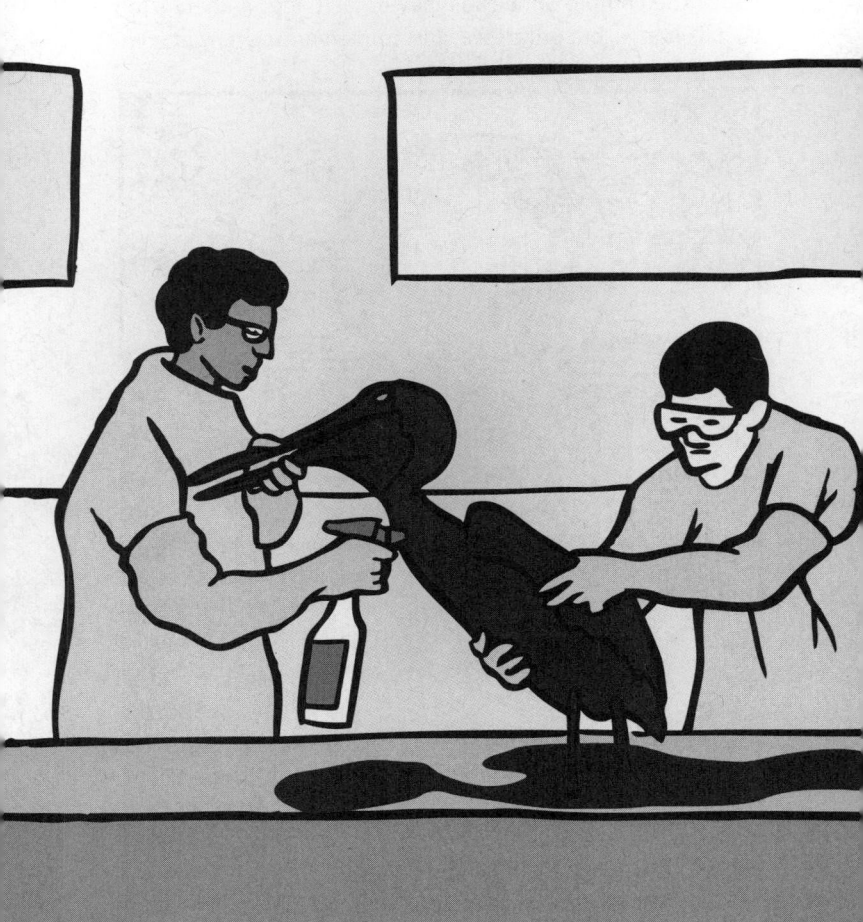

Crisis

One of the justifications for state power is that there have to be institutions to assist people in emergencies. But when disaster strikes, the first priority of the government is not to assist the afflicted, but to reestablish control.

This was clear enough in the aftermath of Hurricane Katrina. Wherever troops could not reassert control immediately, they quarantined a dead zone, denying access to institutional relief groups as well as independent efforts. Corporate media painted this zone in lurid colors—easy enough, as the storm only exacerbated the effects of generations of poverty. Government rhetoric shifted from rescue to repression: as Brigadier General Gary Jones explained, "This place is going to look like Little Somalia . . . This will be a combat operation to get this city under control." New Orleans became a part of the Third World to be occupied and pacified.

The hurricane revealed how tenuous the buffer is between First and Third World. All the conveniences and guarantees of industrial capitalism—the utilities and products that appear as if out of nowhere, the constant flow of information, the protection of the authorities—became health hazards, helpless dependence, and a mix of bureaucracy and violence. Yet when the façade of civil society was torn away, cooperation and compassion actually increased. Despite the efforts of the police and military to control access to the area, a great part of the relief work was carried out autonomously by people who stayed behind or slipped through police lines to help each other.

Some corporate media criticized the state response to the hurricane, but one might ask where this outrage was *before* the storm hit. New Orleans was among the principal ports of the US slave trade, and the descendents of slaves had lived there ever since without much improvement in their living conditions. Poverty rates were among the highest in the US; in the months leading up to the hurricane, ten residents were killed by police officers and two different policemen were indicted for committing rape while in uniform. The skull-and-crossbones logo improvised by officers during the heady days of the post-hurricane occupation made explicit what many in New Orleans already felt: the police formed the vanguard of death, separating people from the resources they needed on a permanent basis.

By interrupting the disaster of everyday life, the hurricane exposed middle-class observers to tragedies to which they were not yet desensitized. In focusing on the flaws of relief efforts, corporate media directed attention away from the ongoing disaster of capitalism and back to the exceptional case of a particular natural disaster. Yet during the hurricane, some impoverished residents of New Orleans may have had *more* access than usual to the things they needed—not because of the efforts of relief agencies, but because the breakdown of control made it possible to take food, water, and clothing that

were otherwise guarded by high prices and men with guns.

After order was restored in New Orleans, things only got worse for the poor. Every crisis offers an opportunity to restructure things; so long as the ones who had power before the crisis retain it, they will set about this in a way that suits their interests. Governments take advantage of crises to break up unruly communities; business interests take advantage of crises to impose more profitable arrangements. Sometimes this can be accomplished simply by standing aside and letting a disaster run its course, then swooping in afterwards; other times, it's necessary to force changes through in the name of maintaining order.

In addition to natural disasters there are also what we might call induced disasters. If the former category includes hurricanes, earthquakes, and pandemics, the latter covers wars, recessions, genocide, and terrorism. It's difficult to say which kind of disaster has inflicted more suffering upon humanity, but as capitalism has spread the latter form has accounted for a greater and greater share of harm.

Like natural disasters, induced disasters appear beyond anyone's control. Who can stop nations from fighting or prevent the market from crashing? Yet such crises would be impossible without the institutions that give rise to them; they only seem inescapable because no one can imagine doing without centralized government or private property. When the International Monetary Fund forces austerity measures on a country, it's not like there's less food, housing, or education to go around than before—the problem is that the current economic system can't distribute access to these according to human need. The same goes for famines that plague one nation while another pays farmers subsidies *not* to grow crops: the means exist to eradicate famine once and for all, but they will never be used for this so long as resources flow according to the laws of profit.

Like natural disasters, induced disasters also offer opportunities for the powerful to secure their interests. After the collapse of communism in the Eastern Bloc countries, advocates of free market capitalism orchestrated the privatization of tremendous swathes of their markets, producing starker inequalities than had existed under communist rule. The authorities can use disasters to strengthen their position even when these are brought about by their adversaries: witness Hitler's use of the attempted burning of the Reichstag to solidify his hold on power in Germany. Likewise, after the attacks of September 11, 2001, the Bush administration took advantage of the opportunity to crack down on domestic dissent and invade Afghanistan and Iraq. The subsequent occupations were an ongoing disaster for both the occupying soldiers and the occupied people, but a tremendous success for Halliburton and Dyncorp.

With incentives like this, disasters are sometimes choreographed in cold blood—such as the distribution of smallpox-infected blankets to Native Americans or the US-backed military coup in Chile. After the damage has been done, the perpetrators may be deposed, disavowed, even charged with war crimes—but the ones who benefit rarely give up the resulting advantages, regardless of how much they wring their hands and use words like "deplorable."

So crises play an essential role in capitalism; sometimes they're even scripted into it. Indeed, crisis management has been adopted as the paradigm for many forms of control. For instance, the Israeli security apparatus, which is emulated by militaries and police worldwide, is built on a model of permanent crisis and permanent intervention.

Under these conditions, real disaster relief would mean not just looting stores, but taking over the factories that produce goods. It would entail commandeering vehicles, food, and weapons—not just to escape from flooded cities, but to carry out a collective jailbreak from this society. It would demand building up networks of mutual aid to enable people to lead lives of their choosing rather than suffering the domination of bosses or poverty.

Precarity and Vertigo

Wherever you are on the pyramid, it only takes a single wrong step to lose your footing—and someone is always ready to take your place.

When it comes to maintaining their positions, the wealthy have the advantage that money tends to make money, while workers have the concessions won by the labor movement: unions, contracts, rights. But as markets globalize and labor-saving technologies shift laborers from manufacturing into the service sector, steady full-time employment is giving way to temporary and part-time work. This takes many different forms: seasonal labor, day labor, temp labor, medical studies. The common denominators are low wages, few rights, few prospects for advancement, no benefits or job security, and great difficulty organizing with other employees.

Harried by debt, with bills coming due monthly and no savings to fall back on, workers survive in a condition of constant uncertainty and pressure. The effects aren't limited to a single class: faced with the prospect of such a precarious existence, even the wealthy live in fear. The stockbrokers who jumped off buildings on Black Monday literally preferred plummeting to their deaths over dropping to a lower economic stratum.

Yet there is something seductive about letting go and dropping out of the rat race, in the same way that a drowning man can be tempted to cease struggling. This is not the way we're supposed to live, always fighting, always calculating. Refusing to compete is a way to affirm values besides those enforced by the market, in an era that offers few alternatives; it can be a means of seeking others who also wish to live in a different world. But those who drop out don't find themselves in another world—they remain in this one, plunging downward.

In a time of constant flux and restructuring, the earth is crowded with isolated human beings. So many people have lost their places in society—not just their jobs, but their social ties, their traditions, their very sense of self. The processes that drive the market have created an enormous population of atomized individuals—refugees without home or homeland, most of whom don't appear in United Nations crisis reports. If there is to be any hope of life after capitalism, we have to find each other and build new connections.

"Anyone whose goal is 'something higher' must expect some day to suffer vertigo. What is vertigo? Fear of falling? Then why do we feel it even when the observation tower comes equipped with a sturdy handrail? No, vertigo is something other than the fear of falling. It is the voice of the emptiness below us which tempts and allures us, it is the desire to fall against which, terrified, we defend ourselves."
– Milan Kundera, *The Unbearable Lightness of Being*

At the nadir of every abyss—another abyss yawns

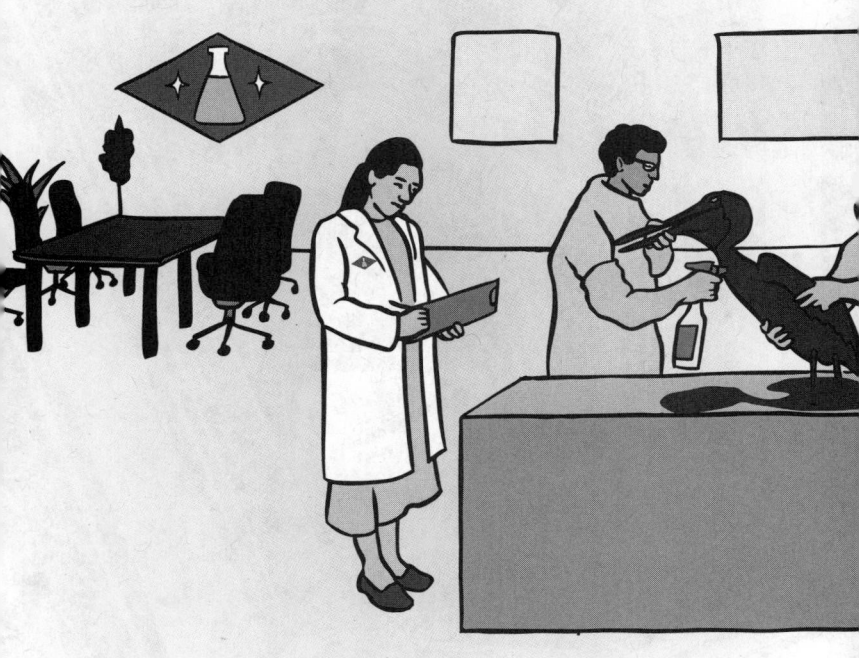

Reformism

The workers' movements of the early 20th century were pacified with labor reforms and bureaucratic unions; those who persisted in calling for revolution were singled out in anti-communist witch hunts. The resistance movements against Pinochet's dictatorship in Chile helped force him to relinquish power, but after the transition to democracy the renegades who went on fighting against the economic policies he'd imposed were ruthlessly repressed by their former fellow dissidents. After one faction of the US animal rights movement shifted to promoting consumer veganism, the other was targeted by a host of repressive measures including the Animal Enterprise Terrorism Act.

Every time people mount a formidable challenge to some aspect of the capitalist system, a version of the same script plays out. The defenders of the status quo placate some of their adversaries, then stop at nothing to crush the ones who won't compromise. Thus the opposition is divided in two by a mixture of seduction and violence, and the ruling order is reconstituted to include a portion of the previous dissidents while the rest are suppressed.

Given this choice, the more sensible ones hurry to reach a settlement rather than risk the full force of repression. Ironically, this option becomes sensible chiefly because so many choose it. Once a critical mass opts to negotiate a truce, all but the most intractable rush to join in like rats leaving a sinking ship. Those who will not—who insist on trying to do away with exploitation and oppression rather than reconciling themselves to lesser degrees of them—are criminalized with new laws, public smear campaigns, and ruthless attacks.

And yet reformists often owe the concessions they receive to those who will not compromise. Liberals and reactionaries allege that confrontational resistance delegitimizes dissent, but in fact it forces the state to legitimize reformists. The black civil rights movement would never have won the gains it did without the implicit threat represented by militants like Malcolm X and later the Black Panthers. Proponents of reform achieve their breakthroughs and accolades as their former comrades are killed or imprisoned—indeed, those breakthroughs and accolades are granted on the condition that they remain silent as the rebels are crushed and written out of history. This gives subsequent generations a false impression of how social change happens, implying that it can only be brought about by petitioning the powerful through the correct institutional channels.

Through this process, the remnants of old resistance movements become intertwined with the ruling social order; this can make things very complicated indeed. For example, the African National Congress, once among the staunchest foes of apartheid in South Africa, now rules the country, presiding over economic inequalities comparable to the racial segregation it once opposed. Many who originally rallied to the ANC banner because of its revolutionary politics now support it even though it has abandoned these; communities that remain in conflict with the South African government find themselves at odds with their former allies.

So pacification may be initiated from unexpected quarters or assume subtle forms. It's not always easy to tell when those who claim to oppose the status quo are actually defending it.

In the US, one of the major factors in the neutralization of potential resistance movements is *funding*. Those who set out to change things must draw resources from somewhere. When nearly everything is privately owned, this means competing on the market, seeking donations, or seizing resources outright. The last option is difficult to sustain, and it's not hard to see how the first two can shape a group's interests. So it is that the wealthy are able to exert disproportionate influence over movements for social change by selective funding.

The structures through which funding is distributed date back over a century to the days when magnates like Rockefeller and Carnegie established foundations. Their goal was to placate the poor and restless while reshaping society according to their interests; philanthropy has a long history as a symptomatic treatment for systemic ills. To this day, tax-deductible donations offer the wealthy a way to dodge the Internal Revenue Service in order to use their money for "charitable" purposes—such as arts programs and right-wing think tanks—that chiefly benefit their class.

Most funding reaches explicitly reactionary organizations, equipping them to work in tandem with government agencies, corporate media outlets, and other institutions to maintain the status quo and the illusion that it is freely chosen. In addition, some trickles down to groups that profess to seek social change, though it brings the class agenda of the funders with it. The reforms sought by the Sierra Club would not fundamentally change how our society relates to the environment any more than the reforms called for by the Humane Society would alter the position of animals relative to human beings. Reforms such as these are chiefly aimed at easing the consciences of middle-class liberals for whom being socially responsible is a consumer option like any other.

The same goes for anti-war coalitions that oppose particular wars without doing anything about the root causes of war and occupation. The protest marshals lining their marches

Don't worry, Horst, I'll explain to them that they're
just going to have to be patient.

are a dead giveaway that the organizers still believe whole-heartedly in top-down control. Thus most non-governmental organizations simply serve to govern society by other means; most non-profit organizations merely ameliorate a system based on profit and exploitation.

Still others set out to achieve real change but are subtly redirected in the process of seeking funding. Those who depend on grants tend to focus on what will impress benefactors, even if they do so unconsciously. Rather than nurturing grass-roots ties, they establish networks within a professional class of organizers and philanthropists; rather than building autonomous social movements, they concentrate on building legitimacy in the eyes of potential patrons. A process of natural selection does away with funding-dependent organizations that won't police themselves. All this reinforces the idea that no one is ready for radical solutions—though those who sponsor the non-profit sector are hardly representative of the general population.

Activists from well-funded groups look at penniless would-be revolutionists with scorn, even confusion. Why can't they get their act together? How can they expect to accomplish anything if they don't toe the line at least a little? Goodness, how *impractical* they are! Don't they know that there are foundations literally *giving away* money, if you just know how to behave?

Some of these activists may think they're pulling one over on their funders, redirecting liberal grant money to subversive purposes. Perhaps they are, but it's not always clear who is scamming whom. Such activists are often as inexperienced as they are passionate, while the ones who write grants are trained professionals with generations of institutional memory to guide them; it would be a mistake to assume they don't know what they're doing.

The most radical groups can still serve a purpose within the economy—by providing free labor, for example. Volunteers are readily given roles responding to the worst effects of capitalism—such as homelessness or oil spills—and thus stabilizing the system itself. These roles can effectively quarantine radicals, causing them to encounter others as victims rather than potential comrades. Shifting from seeking social change to providing social services means you can put in a lifetime of work treating the symptoms without ever making progress against the cause. This may not make the world a better place, but it makes perfect sense as a means of ensuring job security. As capitalist crises beget new markets and new business models, unsavory symbiotic relationships emerge: for example, climate change literally offers job opportunities and salaries via environmentalist NGOs.

Even among those who commit themselves to lifelong struggle, the better-funded reformist organizations eventually reabsorb all but the most recalcitrant; in this way they serve as a final safety net against people turning their full potential against the capitalist system. Progressive NGOs

Bono, old chap, I like the way you think. A little realism can take you far in this business.

offer jobs to the most effective organizers—and what radical doesn't need a job, especially an *ethical* one? Yet the activist who attempts to make a professional career out of saving the world has to confine her self-directed efforts to her spare time, as a hobby. Channeling the majority of her time and energy into her paid work, she eventually gets the impression that her paid work is more *effective.*

Talk of fostering "leadership" often means separating effective organizers from their comrades and teaching them how to achieve *realistic* goals—that is, how to internalize the logic of capitalist reality. Once you see yourself as a leader, you tend to look at the elites of other groups as their legitimate representatives: the homeowners' association in the black neighborhood is seen as speaking for the entire black community, the prominent spokesperson comes to stand in for the social movement. Networks of leaders can string together huge coalitions in such a way that only the elites involved accrue power—this is the accumulation of *political capital.*

As new leaders are "empowered," they subconsciously adopt their own experience of gaining influence as a model of what progress looks like for everyone: social mobility, not the abolition of structural inequalities. But the pyramid of political activism is no different from any other pyramid: there's not enough room for everyone at the top.

Thus the same hierarchies we are fighting reappear within our resistance; often they are imposed by the people who speak most eloquently about resistance, who appear most *qualified* to speak about it. Sometimes such leaders utilize the rhetoric of resisting oppression and privilege to shut down criticism and hamstring real resistance movements. Anything that threatens capitalism probably poses a threat to their leadership roles as well.

In view of all this, it's not enough to ask whether an organization or campaign distributes power down the pyramid—even this may simply be a way of stabilizing the pyramid itself. The question to ask is whether it *contributes to the destruction of the structures that produce the pyramid.* Reformism can be a step towards this, but it can just as easily be a way of putting a stop to it.

Culture and Subculture

Culture—broadly understood as values, practices, ideas and ideologies—is the fabric of social life. From the moment of our birth, it constructs us and we reconstruct it. Our whole society has been remade in the image of the capitalist economy, but it still retains traces from outside its logic. And culture isn't static: as it is constantly reproduced and reinvented, every new generation offers an opportunity to break with the old ways.

Capitalism appears to perpetuate itself independent of culture: it gives the impression that it doesn't need people to buy into it ideologically so long as they have to participate in it to survive. Yet there is always another choice. Millions of people in the so-called New World and elsewhere chose to fight and die rather than survive on its terms. This shows that the "material needs" that drive the economy are still socially produced, just as the obedience it requires is culturally conditioned.

So resisting capitalism isn't just an economic matter but also a cultural one, involving a shift in values and practices. Those who reject exploitation and oppression are bound to appear culturally *different*. This can appear as an external difference—for example, indigenous peoples fighting to retain their ways of life—or it can manifest itself inside capitalist society as *counterculture*. At the same time, culture can appear "different" and even oppositional without actually challenging capitalism at all.

Colonization wiped out or homogenized a vast range of societies, effectively erasing most of the old alternatives to capitalism. As new peoples were pressed into the workforce, capitalists took advantage of cultural differences to divide workers and prevent them from finding common cause. Yet even cultures that have been colonized for hundreds of years can preserve a spark of defiance, and cultural minorities often offer fertile soil for new revolts: for example, the most militant wings of the original US labor movement were based in immigrant communities. The mythology of the United States as a melting pot—a space in which many peoples meet and blend into something new—glorified the project of replacing all these potentially insurgent cultures with a new mass culture.

But this new mass culture could be dangerous, too. Once the wage compromise initiated by Henry Ford stabilized workplace struggles, the front lines of resistance shifted to the terrain of consumption. Mass-produced culture created the possibility of mass refusal, as the colossal social bodies that had coalesced through shared consumer activity rebelled against conformity and alienation. At the beginning of his book, *Do It!*, counterculture icon Jerry Rubin credited the unrest of the 1960s to this phenomenon: "The New Left sprang, a predestined pissed-off child, from Elvis' gyrating pelvis." The generation that started out rebelling against its parents' sexual repression ended up rioting in the streets.

In response, capitalists incorporated these demands for individuality and diversity into the market. This coincided with the shift from straightforward mass production to increasingly diversified consumer goods and identities. Henceforth, in place of mass culture, there would be an ever widening array of subcultures. This might appear to be a return to the era of diversity that preceded mass culture, but there was an important distinction: while ethnic differences predated capitalism, subcultural differences were produced and distributed through the market even when they rejected its values. At the same time, like mass culture, they created new common reference points that cut across older cultural and social divisions.

If Beatlemania exemplified mass culture—selling unprecedented numbers of records, but spinning out of control when millions of fans adopted their idols' countercultural affiliations—the emergence of metal, punk, and hip hop in the 1970s exemplified the "post-Fordist" proliferation of subcultures. There were still superstars, but the music market spread out horizontally around them.

Following the 1970s, almost everyone with confrontational tendencies was effectively quarantined in a distinct subculture. Yet once again, this posed new risks to capitalism, as it was easier for radicals to gain leverage in these smaller milieus. Early hip hop established a direct link with the black power struggles of the 1960s, emboldening a new generation of the excluded. Underground punk bands released their own records and established their own venues, setting up an alternative economy based in "do-it-yourself" networks and anticapitalist values. This was a breakthrough in that they were using formats that had been largely off limits to the working class to spread subversive messages; at the same time, they were pioneering and validating a new form of entrepreneurship, paving the way for less politicized entrepreneurs.

This combination of anticapitalist values with small-scale capitalism was fragile but potent. As the market spread Western culture around the world, new countercultures connected anticapitalist currents from Chile to Turkey and the Philippines, helping to give an international character to the next generation's forms of resistance. This peaked at the turn of the century with a wave of protests against corporate globalization, in which fierce youth countercultures helped give a militant edge to a movement that also included indigenous peoples, NGOs, and the remnants of organized labor.

In the early 21st century, new technologies universalized the network-based structures that had formed the backbone of the do-it-yourself underground. The internet made everyone with a Facebook page an "independent artist," simultaneously embracing and superseding the promise of do-it-yourself culture. The new ease and speed with which culture could be consumed rendered subcultures transient and superficial. This drained the underground of its former political content, leaving it an aesthetic shell.

Today, the dominant medium of youth culture is not vinyl records but Youtube videos: instantaneous and forgettable. The previous generation's subcultures are atomizing into smaller and smaller sub-niches. This is a subset of the atomization of the exploited and excluded generally. Consumer taste no longer tends to create coherent social bodies likely to develop radical conceptions of their interests. Instead, radicalism itself has become a sort of niche, while the newest subcultures are based in the virtual reality of the internet.

What do we still have in common in this era of cultural fragmentation? If nothing else, we're connected by what we've lost. We're all denied influence over the world around us except insofar as we can turn ourselves or others into merchandise. We're all subject to rules and regulations most of us have no say in devising. We all live in the shadow of superstars—even superstars live in the shadow of their own images—in a world in which reality is subordinate to representation. We're all evaluated according to the norms of the market; if we want to fulfill our potential, it seems we can only do so within it. In place of the shared sense of belonging culture used to provide, we share a universal dispossession, imposed chiefly by our common willingness to tolerate it.

None of this is particularly new, but it has never been so universal. And one other thing has changed: when people revolt somewhere, everyone instantly hears about it everywhere.

CULTURES OF RESISTANCE
SUBCULTURES OF RESISTANCE

The economists promised us endless growth. Everyone would have his own property, his own investments—everyone would be a capitalist. We took out loans to get degrees for jobs that didn't exist, took on mortgages we couldn't afford, racked up credit card bills pretending that we, too, were middle class.

Now it's clear there's no room for us at the top. Capitalism is a pyramid scheme that has run out of ways to expand. People are rioting in Greece, striking in Quebec, overthrowing governments in North Africa. Revolt is ricocheting back and forth across the world as the effects of the recession sink in. This wave of uprisings will reach the US last of all, but it's on its way. The ruling order will seem unshakable until the day before it collapses.

Italy, December 2010

II. The Resistance

USA, right now

We don't have to live like this.

Some social conventions, such as private property, create imbalances in power and access to resources. Others don't. There are ways to meet our needs without buying and selling. There are ways to relate to others without trying to profit at their expense.

This is hard to believe now that capitalism has colonized nearly every aspect of our lives. But there are still countless examples of other ways to do things. For production, think of barn-raising events, in which communities come together for a day to build structures that would otherwise take months, or open-source software, in which programs are created and refined cooperatively by all who use them. For distribution, think of libraries, which can stock a lot more than books, or file-sharing, in which those who need a file self-organize its circulation. For relationships, think of healthy friendships and family ties, in which everyone is invested in everyone else's welfare, or parties and festivals in which even strangers enjoy each other's participation.

None of these models promotes selfishness or discourages effort. All of them undermine the notion of scarcity: the more people participate, the more everyone benefits. There must be ways to extend such formats into other spheres of life.

Of course, the idea of reorganizing our whole society is daunting. From this standpoint, we can't imagine what it will entail or what the outcome will look like. But we can *begin*.

Abolishing private property surely involves challenges and drawbacks of its own, but these could hardly be worse than the effects of global capitalism. We've all heard of the so-called tragedy of the commons, the idea that people can't be trusted to take care of resources for which all are equally responsible. There is a grain of truth to this: the real tragedy was that the commons were privatized, that people failed to protect them against the ones who snatched them up. If we want to do away with capitalism, we have to learn how to defend ourselves from those who would impose the *tragedy of property.*

So much of the world has been taken from us that it would be disorienting to find ourselves suddenly sharing it all again. We can get a hint of what this might be like by looking at recent uprisings in which people created autonomous zones outside capitalism: Oaxaca 2006, Athens 2008, Cairo 2011. The exhilaration of taking over and repurposing spaces, of acting spontaneously en masse, has very little in common with day-to-day life in capitalist society. Dismantling capitalism doesn't just mean holding material goods in common, but rediscovering each other and ourselves—embracing a totally different way of being in the world.

Denmark, October 2006

CAPITALISM
IS DOOMED

Madison, February 2011

Capitalism is headed for catastrophe.

However stable things may seem in some parts of the world, we're entering a new era of crisis and uncertainty.

Capitalism has never been as pervasive as it is now. The previous generation experienced *alienation,* suffering from the dissonance between their roles in production and their sense of themselves; the current generation is characterized by *identification* with economic roles that are diffusing into every sphere of life. Yet at the moment of its triumph, capitalism is more precarious than ever.

All the peace treaties of the 20th century have expired. The higher wages Henry Ford offered his workers have vanished with the jobs themselves; unions have been outflanked by globalization; the socialist nations of the East have transitioned to free-market capitalism while the social democracies of the West are being dismantled. But those compromises weren't just ways to avoid confrontation—they also served to perpetuate capitalism. Ford's wage increases enabled his employees to buy products and keep the pyramid scheme expanding; unions prevented capitalists from impoverishing their consumer base. Now that capitalists have abandoned their former means of co-optation and *self-perpetuation,* the future is up for grabs. The old alternatives have been discredited, but new revolutionary ideas are bound to come to the fore.

Capitalism is predicated on the endless accumulation of profit, but this profit has to come from somewhere. Once you bleed workers dry, the rate of profit falls, causing the market to stagnate. Until recently, it was possible to solve this problem by constantly drawing in new resources and populations. Now capitalism has spread across the entire world, connecting everyone and rendering any crisis truly global. At the same time, industrial production is reaching its ecological limits, while technological progress has rendered much of the workforce redundant, creating an increasingly restless surplus population.

Capitalism has been on the brink of crisis for decades now. Extending credit to a broader and broader range of the exploited has been a way of keeping up consumption while the workforce gets poorer. Investors have shifted their wealth into financial markets, hoping to profit on speculation now that profits from material production have plateaued. The vast majority of innovation has centered in new *immaterial* markets: information, branding, social networking. All this has only succeeded in delaying the day of reckoning.

The financial downturn of 2008 wasn't a fluke, but a sign of things to come. It's not simply a matter of waiting until things return to normal. The next phase of the crisis might not hit the US for years or decades, but it's on its way. Already, the capitalist economy is barely able to offer people decent jobs, let alone meaningful lives; even measured by its own materialistic criteria, it isn't working.

Likewise, it's no coincidence that you're reading this book right now. Insofar as the economy is the concrete manifestation of the values and hierarchies of our society, a financial crisis heralds a crisis of faith in the system itself. A new wave of unrest is bound to arise.

In periods of turmoil, people reevaluate their assumptions and values. Of course, we can't be sure what the outcome will be; even if capitalism collapses, what comes next could be *even worse*. Right now it's extremely important to set positive examples of what it means to resist and what the alternatives to capitalism might be. During social upheavals, people's notion of what is *possible* can shift very quickly, but their notion of what is *desirable* usually changes more slowly. This explains why grassroots uprisings often settle for demands that are much less radical than the forms adopted by the uprisings themselves: it takes a long time for our imaginations to catch up with reality.

If it's quiet right now where you live, that doesn't mean it always will be. Think ahead to the upheavals on the horizon: when they arrive, what will you wish you had done to prepare? How can you maximize the likelihood that they will turn out for the best?

We don't offer the only road out of capitalism, but we believe ours is the most inviting one. We don't propose corporate feudalism, ethnic warfare, concentration camps, ecological collapse, global famine, or nuclear war. A few decades of pitched social conflict are nothing compared to the catastrophes that will ensue if we don't take the initiative. Make no mistake, the world is going to change. It's up to us whether it will change for better or worse.

We're not peddling a utopia. We simply want to learn from the practices that worked to keep our species a healthy part of the ecosystem for the last million years, in hopes that we might survive at least a few thousand more. This humble aspiration places us in direct conflict with the current social order.

Canada, June 2010

Half measures won't save us.

What could end the tyranny of the market? We don't have any easy answers, but we're convinced this is the most important question. Half measures are seductive because they seem more feasible than structural change; in fact, it would be easier to overthrow capitalism altogether than to alter its effects while leaving the causes intact. To get started, we can identify some approaches that don't work, then advance hypotheses about what might.

Charity won't solve the problems created by capitalism; neither will volunteer work or single-issue campaigns. We could spend our entire lives treating the symptoms one by one without making any progress towards a cure.

Painting capitalism "green" won't make it sustainable. Neither will limiting our consumption. When the economy rewards destructive behavior, accepting voluntary limitations just means ceding power to less scrupulous competitors. Likewise, as long as those incentives remain, only the most autocratic government could prevent people from pursuing them. Ecological collapse or ecological fascism—there must be another choice.

Unions won't rescue us from capitalism. When corporations can move jobs around the planet at will, it's no longer effective to resist one workplace at a time, or even one country at a time. Even if we could protect the rights of workers in a particular industry, that would simply give them an advantage to defend against others among the exploited and excluded; we need structures for dismantling the pyramid itself, not for protecting the interests of specific groups inside it.

New technologies won't render capitalism obsolete. Filesharing, free software, and social networking don't change the material inequalities at the base. As long as the economy dominates our lives, participatory formats will just integrate us into it more seamlessly.

There's no way to escape capitalism on an individual basis; there's no outside to withdraw to. Crime can offer an advantage to the exploited and excluded, but it doesn't point beyond the logic of the system; successful hackers and scam artists often end up working for security corporations or the FBI.

So long as they don't confront capitalism itself, identity-based liberation movements won't put an end to injustice and inequality. Being exploited by people like yourself is hardly an improvement on being exploited by people different from you. Even if we could all experience equal opportunity within capitalism—even if domination and exploitation could be distributed without reference to race, gender, or any other axis of oppression—capitalism itself would still be oppressive.

Government reforms won't cure capitalism. They might temporarily offset its effects, but the property-owning class always has an advantage when it comes to using the structures of the state. Even if anticapitalists took over and established a brand new government, the most they could do would be to control capital themselves, becoming a new capitalist class. Communists already did that in the 20th century with catastrophic results. At best, government solutions could strive towards the ideal of everyone sharing control of capital through the coercive apparatus of the state; but even if that were possible, it would only be a new sort of hell: an authoritarian system without authorities.

Self-management and "direct democracy" won't suffice to convey us beyond capitalism. Even without bosses or rulers, capitalist institutions will go on producing the same effects if we keep using them for their intended purposes—the same way the state apparatus continues *ruling* even without monarchs. If we take over our workplaces but go on *working* in them, if we still have to go through the economy for everything we need, we will continue suffering the same disconnection from ourselves and the world around us.

Even in the midst of catastrophe, there's no guarantee capitalism will fall on its own. For over a century and a half, Marxists have promised that capitalism would collapse once the "material conditions" ripened sufficiently; but every crisis has left capitalism stabler than ever. Next time it's in danger of breaking down, we have to seize the opportunity to interpose a different way of life.

There's no way around it—if we want fundamental change, we have to abolish private ownership of capital. This is not just an economic and political transformation, but also a social and cultural one. It cannot be imposed from above, but must be carried out by a critical mass prepared to defend themselves.

We can't know whether capitalism will fall in our lifetime, but we know it will fall. In the meantime, we can establish anticapitalism in the popular imagination as the opposition to the present order, so people don't gravitate to reformist or reactionary programs. We can also shake faith in the capitalist system, showing that it is neither the best way of structuring our lives, nor the only one possible, nor even stable or reliable. Capitalism is a spell: it can be broken.

Egypt, February 2011

Keep updating your strategies and tactics.

To recapitulate: starting early in the industrial revolution, people initiated resistance on the basis of common roles in production, organizing unions in their workplaces and forging subversive relationships in their neighborhoods. After the labor compromises of the early 20th century, the front lines of resistance shifted to the terrain of consumption, as the alienation of mass-produced society gave rise to mass unrest. As consumer markets diversified, the latter became more and more subculturally specific.

Today we're fragmented spatially, socially, and culturally, but we're also more interconnected than ever before. Whatever the advantages of the previous formats for struggle, they've reached their limits; they may still be useful, but they're unlikely to produce anything new. We shouldn't evaluate new formats according to the criteria of the old ones, but rather according to how effectively they make use of new opportunities.

For example, at the end of the 20th century, an international movement arose around protesting at the summits of trade organizations such as the International Monetary Fund. Dubbed the "anti-globalization movement" by pundits loath to say *anticapitalism,* this movement attempted to block a new wave of capitalist deregulation. Anticapitalist critics contended that such "summit-hopping" failed to build long-term local struggles; this was true, but in an era of cosmopolitanism and transience international mobilizations took advantage of what people were already doing, while local organizing had to pull against the current. Insofar as they inhibited corporations from imposing worse conditions on workers, summit protests filled a role that unions no longer could on their own.

The same goes for the critique that subculturally-based outreach confines resistance to narrow social groups. Once again, this is obviously true, but it doesn't account for why these efforts have recently been so effective compared to other forms of organizing. Explicitly anticapitalist unions may still play an important role in resistance, but if people come to them through subcultural channels as often as through workplace organizing, we have to analyze this and strategize accordingly. The point is not to return to the strengths of the old tactics, but to transcend the shortcomings of the new ones.

In the US, it seems that production and consumption no longer create massive social bodies likely to conceive of their interests outside of capitalism. On the contrary, both have been structured so as not to constitute coherent social bodies at all. This is not necessarily for the worst: if we want to abolish capitalism, it might be better not to conceptualize ourselves according to our roles within it. But how else can people come together to resist?

It seems likely that the next phase of struggles will center around the terrain of *information*. Just as the factory system mass-produced an entire social structure alongside material goods, the new social formations are shaped by the ways we are informed. Now that much of the human race is extraneous to production, the main thing that binds us to the current social order is the way it structures our interactions and our notions of what is possible. The new participatory media serve to keep a redundant population

busy competing for *attention* inside a capitalist framework, a process that subtly dictates what we can imagine.

Fighting on the terrain of information doesn't just mean blocking websites, as the decentralized group Anonymous did in retaliation for the crackdown on Wikileaks. This terrain extends beyond the internet and cell phones to all the other structures via which people jointly construct their conception of reality. The languages and frameworks through which our species attributes meaning are now at stake: we have to create new connections between people, new networks through which information can flow and people can respond to the world around them. The futher offline these networks extend, the more likely they are to remain under our control.

This might appear to be a rearguard struggle: capitalism has already conquered the entire planet and now we're fighting in our very last redoubt, our own mental spaces and social relationships. But in every struggle, the entirety of the capitalist system comes back into question. This is especially true now that new forms of self-organization can spread almost instantaneously. In this context, sparks of resistance can transcend the limits of activism and subculture to catalyze full-scale revolts.

As we were completing this book, rebellions broke out throughout Tunisia, Egypt, and other parts of the Middle East. A new generation, impoverished and uprooted yet linked by new technologies, initiated a wave of leaderless revolt. This began at the margins, yet as soon as it became clear that it had any hope of success, the rest of the population swiftly joined in. The Egyptian government shut down the internet and cell phone networks in response, but this only enraged the population further. This uprising has yet to assume anticapitalist forms, but it offers a glimpse of what an anticapitalist revolution might entail; more specifically, it underscores how central communications technologies and social networks will be to any major uprising to come.

In the future we'll probably see governments attempt to shape the architecture of communication so that it's unnecessary to shut down the internet. Corporations like Google will subtly direct the flow of attention, promoting certain forms of protest and suppressing others. The extent to which we can keep channels open for free communication will determine the prospects for liberation.

Fight where you stand.

Whatever your position on the pyramid—whether you're a high school student, a temp worker, a stagehand with union benefits, a lawyer, or homeless and unemployed—you can fight where you are. You're most likely to be effective when you confront the outrages you experience personally on the terrain you know best.

Insofar as our lives are colonized, we have to take the roles that are forced on us as our first point of departure for resistance. It's easy to confine resistance to our leisure time, to make it something *additional*—a meeting packed in at the end of the workday, a bumper sticker. This corresponds with a tendency to fight for causes outside our day-to-day lives. The advantage of the union model is that it takes the daily regimen imposed on workers and turns it into a site for organizing and confrontation. If a conventional union isn't appropriate in your context, you may have to experiment with other formats: a self-defense league, a thieves' ring, a secret society for revolutionary consciousness.

Capitalism isn't just what happens at work. We can also resist in the rest of our daily lives—defending our neighborhoods against gentrification, occupying foreclosed homes, draining our creditors to the limit and declaring bankruptcy. Collective forms of resistance can be more difficult in consumption than production, but they're possible: take over spaces and use them for public events, go to an expensive affair en masse and force your way in without paying, go to the grocery store and do the same thing on the way out. The more our livelihoods depend on resistance rather than submission, the more fiercely we'll fight.

Seattle, May 2012

Being excluded is also a role that can be refused. You don't have to have a *job* operating the means of production to be entitled to seize them, any more than you have to live in a shopping district to be entitled to loot it. As more and more people are forced to the margins, the role the marginalized must play in resistance becomes more and more central.

As they say on the basketball court, *play your position*. Redirect resources and information to those who can use them more effectively than you can. When people "get serious" about fighting capitalism, they often tend to remove themselves from their previous position within it—quitting jobs, dropping out of school, ceasing to participate in processes rather than *interrupting* them. This serves capitalists just fine—one of the functions of the surplus population is to contain all who would cause trouble if they could. It's better to go on the offensive. Don't quit your job—wait until the boss is most vulnerable and go on strike, inviting everyone to join you. Don't drop out of school and ship off to some activist campaign—organize walkouts and teach-ins, put together a student group that can channel funds off campus, try to carry out an occupation. When they fire or expel you, you'll be entitled to move on with your life.

There's no moral high ground in capitalism: it's not more ethical to be further down the pyramid. Trying to appease your conscience isn't likely to do anyone else a lot of good. Likewise, let others play their positions—don't waste energy judging them. Even lawyers and professors can play an important role if they can get over themselves. We don't gain anything from moralistic one-upmanship; the point isn't to be *right,* but to be *dangerous*. When we split into rival factions, we save capitalists the trouble of dividing and distracting us.

Every position on the pyramid is a compromise—but choose your compromise carefully. Where you're located will determine what you experience and whom you identify with, inevitably shaping your interests. How you acquire resources will frame your values and your conception of human nature. If you manage to secure a high-paying job to raise funds for projects, for example, you may eventually lose touch with others in less advantageous positions—or simply lose faith that they know how to "get anything done."

Fight alongside others with their best interests at heart, but don't approach resistance as a sort of volunteer work you carry out on their behalf. Forget about trying to identify "the most revolutionary class" or finding someone worse off than yourself to be an "ally" to. If you don't experience others' struggles *as your own struggle,* you'll probably be an erratic ally. The best assistance you can provide to anyone is to threaten the power structure, showing that everyone has a stake in fighting for themselves.

Not that you should take your privileges for granted; on the contrary, refusing your role means rejecting these as well. For example, white protesters aren't *really* interrupting the functioning of capitalism until they force the police to treat them the way delinquents of color are treated. But you'll be most effective enabling others like yourself to revolt, not acting as a foot soldier in someone else's campaign. Whatever it was that pushed you over the edge, make sure that happens to everyone like you.

The point of all this isn't just to get a little revenge or gain advantages you wouldn't have in the economy otherwise, but above all to make connections, to broaden your ties and deepen your skillsets. Start out with a few friends, people that you trust. Get used to coming up with a plan and carrying it out, to reacting to things that anger or sadden you, to *disobeying.* As you find others doing the same thing, you'll build up networks that can swing into action together.

As soon as people see that *something else* really is possible, they find themselves making decisions in a different context. Between upheavals, we can set an example of what it looks like to resist; when things heat up, it'll catch on.

UK, November 2010

Spread narratives that legitimize revolt.

Everyone wants things to be different, but nobody's sure what to do. Even those who have resolved themselves to open warfare aren't sure where to start or how to be sure others will join in with them.

This is why it's so important when something occurs that gives people a common rallying point. When Alexis Grigoropoulos was murdered by policemen in December 2008, all Greece erupted in revolt. In November 2010, tens of thousands rallied against a new law that would raise tuition in the UK. In both of these cases, radicals finally had a narrative that the general population found convincing across cultural and political lines, legitimizing forms of resistance that many people had never imagined themselves participating in.

Usually, these rallying points are reactive, responding to some new injustice that exceeds even the level of abuse people have come to take for granted. It can be easy for people to agree that they oppose new outrages, but difficult for them to imagine a positive alternative. Legitimacy itself is socially constructed so as to be out of reach of those who would resist; for example, the excluded can claim no "legitimate territory" on which to defend their rights. You can counter these limitations by propagating narratives that go deeper than police misconduct or unfair legislation, offering more fundamental critiques and more transformative visions.

Make a practice of *acting* on these narratives: ideas lack force until people see others behaving as if they are *real*.

Look for vulnerabilities and fault lines in the current configurations of power. Power is distributed unevenly now, but it's also distributed in different currencies—money, attention, social clout—that aren't perfectly interchangeable and don't behave according to the same laws. In the coming conflicts, some of the fault lines—and some of the advantages we can gain—will probably open up around the tensions between these different currencies.

Find ways of fighting that spread.

How does one form of resistance spread or contribute to other forms of resistance? This will determine how effective it can ultimately be. The most decisive aspect of each act of defiance is its relationship to other such acts.

Those who struggle against the constraints of capitalism must come to identify with everyone else who struggles. If they do not, even if they are effective, capitalists will neutralize them by granting their demands at others' expense; at most, they could simply replace the previous ruling class without transforming the system itself.

You can't measure the strength of a revolt the way you would measure the strength of a police department. The force of insurrection is social, not military: the question is how infectious it is, how far it extends into the general population, how much it transforms relationships. Popular uprisings can triumph over much better equipped armies if they retain their popular character. Once the sides become fixed and the scope of the uprising is determined, however, it becomes safe for rulers to rely on brute force once more.

Therefore don't let your foes isolate you from others like yourself, don't get quarantined in subcultural niches, don't let radicals impose obscure points of reference on you that will just make it harder to communicate with society at large. It isn't movements themselves that make social change, but rather *contagious examples of transformation*. That means that

New York, December 2011

people actually in the midst of transformation have more to offer to the project of revolution than partisans of revolution who have not changed in thirty years. The former may not have thought through all their politics and tactics yet, but their inconsistency and awkwardness are balanced out by flexibility, momentum, and optimism, not to mention the relationships they have with people who haven't yet chosen a side. Once their new identities as radicals have crystallized, the roles they can play in social upheavals will be less and less dynamic. They can still fight, of course, perhaps with increasing expertise, but only from a fixed position.

Greece, December 2008

Find ways of fighting that create access to resources outside capitalism.

When it comes to evaluating a tactic or strategy, one of the most important questions is whether it secures more opportunities and resources. Sometimes it can be worth taking a loss to accomplish a particular goal, but once you overextend it can be very difficult to recover. Many projects ultimately founder because they fail to recoup the resources invested in them: you can't carry on an exhausting struggle indefinitely without deriving the wherewithal for it from somewhere.

But if a way of fighting does secure resources, it's just as important to ask *how* it makes them available, how they will circulate. If we don't want to reproduce capitalist property relations, we have to provide for material needs in ways that create other relationships to goods. Resistance is only *anticapitalist* insofar as it immediately establishes these relationships. If the resources we seize still function inside the framework of private property, we can expect the same dynamics to arise inside our own circles that we see in the capitalist economy.

On the other hand, in building new infrastructures, we can demonstrate another way of life, giving people reason to invest themselves in fighting for it. It's challenging to do this when there is so much pressure to privatize everything, but in times when capitalist control breaks down it becomes much easier. We should be ready to seize any opportunity to establish forms of wealth that can be held in common.

Piracy was so effective four centuries ago because in the relative safety of the high seas, it was easy enough for sailors to depose their commanders and take over their ships. The ship represented society in miniature, beyond the reach of the armed forces that maintained the delicate balance of power on land. As soon as sailors mutinied, their first order of business was to draw up new terms of agreement, collectivizing everything on board before setting out to make war on the old order. This form of revolt could spread by cellular division, when a crew split up into two groups; by viral attack, when pirates seized another vessel and liberated the crew; by contagion, when a sailor who had been a pirate signed on with a new vessel; and by rumor, when sailors heard about other pirate revolts and resolved to try it themselves. What sites could serve as the pirate ships of our era? What spaces and resources could be seized and turned against a society based on private ownership?

In addition to collectivizing access to resources immediately, we need ways of fighting that redistribute power itself. To defend themselves against external foes and internal power grabs, insurgent communities need to establish multiple power structures that can counterbalance each other and continuously undermine new hierarchies. There are no shortcuts to freedom; political parties and leaders can't obtain it for us, but only take it from us. If we aren't careful, we could overthrow all the governments of the world and occupy all its workplaces without getting any closer to assuming control of our own destinies.

In the long run, the point is not to make sure *things* are distributed equally, but to establish a relationship to material goods that enables all of us to realize our potential as we see fit. We have to stop engaging with ourselves and each other according to our roles in capitalist society and create new conceptions of what life could be.

Mexico, November 2006

Be ready for a long struggle.

It may not be apparent when things are about to change. The more precarious the old order becomes, the more aggressively it will assert its permanence. A regime that can't afford to show its weakness will avoid compromise at any cost.

In this context, it might not be possible to achieve intermediary goals. Resistance may seem more and more divorced from effectiveness, more and more "irrational," until it finally reaches a critical point.

This makes it more important to focus on the *content* of resistance than on its immediate efficacy. Does it create new relationships between people, new ways of relating to material goods? Does it demonstrate values that point beyond capitalism? Forget about whether it achieves its ostensible demands—does it give rise to new struggles, to new *unruliness*?

As work becomes at once more temporary and more invasive, shifting swiftly around the world and extending into every aspect of life, labor struggles may involve fighting in spaces we think of as far from the workplace. This doesn't mean we should abandon workplace struggle itself, though we may have to reconceptualize what we're trying to achieve with it and how we evaluate its effectiveness so it can play a role in the new forms of conflict.

Every time we invent a new way of fighting, we change the terrain, opening up unforeseen possibilities. We may ultimately lose the battle, but we produce a new social current that can give rise to more fighters and future innovations. We should be prepared to fight over years and decades without growing disheartened. We also need to be prepared to stay the course in the face of sudden changes of context, such as the attacks of September 11, 2001 or the election of Obama; the defenders of capitalism will surely spring their most confusing surprises on us when the war enters its final rounds.

Even when a sudden upheaval finally takes us by surprise, it will only open a new phase of struggle that will surely last the rest of our lives. Shifting from capitalism to other frameworks is bound to be a difficult and protracted process.

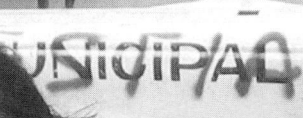

Mexico, September 2006

Mexico, November 2006

Change must go to the roots.

When one power structure collapses, the fragments of old hierarchies that remained within it can reconstitute themselves. For example, immediately after Hurricane Katrina hit New Orleans, a mix of off-duty police officers and vigilantes ran the streets; if one of the tasks of the police is to control the movements of black and brown people, vigilantes can maintain this function even when the entire legal apparatus breaks down.

Alongside every institution, currency, or form of hierarchy, there are the subtle values and practices that enable it to function. Just as nothing could serve as capital without the convention of private property, police departments would be impossible without the conventions of *authority* and *duty*. These aren't just abstractions, but concrete relationships people participate in throughout their lives—this is why people experience them as *real* even though they are socially constructed. Police set a model for what it means to wield power: children grow up playing with action figures, adults *police* each other in a thousand different ways. This shapes our imaginations so that even when we set out to liberate ourselves we often take on familiar oppressive roles.

Just as individuals can be interchangeable within institutions, institutions can be interchangeable in fulfilling certain *functions*. Beside policing we could identify many other functions, less obviously oppressive but no less central to the workings of capitalism. If we want to transform our society, we must not only overturn institutions but also identify the functions they serve, lest we end up taking on these roles ourselves. Even without capital or police, entirely new currencies might arise to impose oppression and alienation.

There's no reason to believe the downfall of capitalism will automatically bring about a free world. That part is up to us.

"What does it really mean to be useful?
Today's world, just as it is, contains the
sum of the utility of all people of all times.
Which implies: the highest morality
consists in being useless."

– Milan Kundera, *Immortality*

"At this historical conjuncture of crisis, rage, and the bank-ruptcy of institutions, the only thing that can bring about a social revolution is the total rejection of work. When street fighting takes place in streets dark from the strike at the Electricity Company—when clashes occur amid tons of uncollected rubbish—when trolleys and buses shut down streets to block off the police—when striking teachers light

up their revolting pupils' molotov cocktails—then we will be finally able to say: 'Ruffians, the days of your society are numbered; we weighed its joys and justices and found them all too little.'"

– statement from the occupation of the Athens School of Economics and Business, December 2008

Greece, December 2008

Bibliography

We've chosen to forego formal citations for this project; in the Google era, it should be easy enough to follow up on any of our claims. This opens a host of questions that usually go unacknowledged in texts about economics. How do certain forms of corroboration benefit from and reinforce academic legitimacy, itself a currency of power? How seriously do we take our subjective experiences relative to the facts and figures of the academy? Who benefits from this, and whom does it silence?

We've drawn on more sources than we could enumerate, but here are a few good starting points →

Mariarosa Dalla Costa and Selma James, *The Power of Women and the Subversion of the Community*

Mike Davis, *Planet of Slums*

Guy Debord, *The Society of the Spectacle*

Barbara Ehrenreich and Deirdre English, *Witches, Midwives, and Nurses*

Endnotes, *Endnotes 2: Misery and the Value Form*

Silvia Federici, *Caliban and the Witch*

Eduardo Galeano, *Open Veins of Latin America*

INCITE! Women of Color Against Violence, *The Revolution Will Not Be Funded: Beyond the Non-Profit Industrial Complex*

Peter Linebaugh and Marcus Rediker, *The Many-Headed Hydra: The Hidden History of the Revolutionary Atlantic*

Fredy Perlman, *Against His-Story, Against Leviathan!* and *The Reproduction of Daily Life*

Prole.info, *Abolish Restaurants*

Upton Sinclair, *The Jungle*

Émile Zola, *Germinal*

This book is set entirely in the typeface RePublic, released by the Suitcase Type Foundry, including its *orderly and inviting italic*, and its **pleasantly fanatical bold condensed**. Originally created by Stanislav Marso in 1955 for a Czech State Department of Culture contest to select the official typeface for the state-run newspaper—which it went on to win—it was revived, expanded, and reworked in 2003 by Tomáš Brousil into a dazzlingly complete OpenType font (*see ffk ligature, really*). Designed to deliver perfect legibility even in adverse printing conditions, on modern presses it delivers an exquisite reading experience while presenting a nuanced beauty to be found in its soft corners and congenial contrast in stroke.

Crimethink designates a kind of activity rather than a body of theory: the practice of subverting control and escaping constraints.

CrimethInc. is a secret society pledged to this activity—one among many.